# ROUTLEDGE LIBRARY EDITIONS: ETHICS

Volume 6

# KNOWING BETTER

# KNOWING BETTER
## An Account of Akrasia

EUNICE BELGUM

LONDON AND NEW YORK

First published in 1990 by Garland Publishing Inc.

This edition first published in 2021
by Routledge
2 Park Square, Milton Park, Abingdon, Oxon OX14 4RN

and by Routledge
52 Vanderbilt Avenue, New York, NY 10017

*Routledge is an imprint of the Taylor & Francis Group, an informa business*

© 1977 Eunice Belgum

All rights reserved. No part of this book may be reprinted or reproduced or utilised in any form or by any electronic, mechanical, or other means, now known or hereafter invented, including photocopying and recording, or in any information storage or retrieval system, without permission in writing from the publishers.

*Trademark notice*: Product or corporate names may be trademarks or registered trademarks, and are used only for identification and explanation without intent to infringe.

*British Library Cataloguing in Publication Data*
A catalogue record for this book is available from the British Library

ISBN: 978-0-367-85624-3 (Set)
ISBN: 978-1-00-305260-9 (Set) (ebk)
ISBN: 978-0-367-47435-5 (Volume 6) (hbk)
ISBN: 978-1-00-303561-9 (Volume 6) (ebk)

**Publisher's Note**
The publisher has gone to great lengths to ensure the quality of this reprint but points out that some imperfections in the original copies may be apparent.

**Disclaimer**
The publisher has made every effort to trace copyright holders and would welcome correspondence from those they have been unable to trace.

# Knowing Better

*An Account of Akrasia*

*Eunice Belgum*

GARLAND PUBLISHING
NEW YORK & LONDON
1990

**Library of Congress Cataloging-in-Publication Data**

Knowing better: an account of akrasia / Eunice Belgum.
p. cm. — (Harvard dissertations in philosophy)
Thesis (doctoral)—Harvard University, 1976.
Includes bibliographical references.
ISBN 0-8240-3185-7
1. Aristotle. Nicomachean ethics. 2. Ethics. 3. Good and evil. 4. Free will and determinism. I. Title. II. Title: Akrasia. III. Series.
B430.Z7B44    1990
170—dc20    89-49390

*All volumes printed on acid-free, 250-year-life paper*
*Manufactured in the United States of America*

Design by Julie Threlkeld

# *Introduction*

It is an honor, but also a great sadness, to introduce Eunice Belgum's dissertation. I met Eunice my first days in graduate school: we fell into lively discussions, frequently as disputatious as they were affectionate, that continued for many years, and that made for stimulating philosophy and deep friendship. Her sudden and untimely death in 1977 at the age of thirty-one was a terrible loss to all who knew her, as to the profession generally.

Eunice was born in 1946 in Brooklyn, New York, where she lived for ten years until her family moved to Fargo, North Dakota. She did her undergraduate work at St. Olaf College in Minnesota, spending her senior year at Oxford, after which she proceeded to graduate work in philosophy at Harvard. From 1974 until 1976, she taught at Trinity College in Hartford, Connecticut, and then at the College of William and Mary in Virginia, until her death. Her primary interests in philosophy were always in ethics and moral psychology, although toward the end of her life they were becoming increasingly focused upon the then just emerging areas of medical ethics and feminist philosophy. She was an early and active member of the Society for Women in Philosophy, and was one of the first to develop (with Professor Jim Harris at William and Mary) courses on the philosophy of sex and gender. After her death, a memorial fund was established in her name at St. Olaf College for annual lectures there, a series that continues to the present day.

Although outwardly she appeared quiet and soft-spoken, she had an unusually strong and independent mind. In graduate school, she was more resistant than I to the then influential views of Wittgenstein, according to which traditional philosophical problems were due largely to, as it were, bad grammar. She gradually convinced me that many philosophical problems have less to do with language than with genuine tensions between different claims we make about the world, particularly, as will emerge below, between the claims of theory and the "intuitive" claims we make in presumed pre-theoretic innocence. She was especially sensitive to the tensions in ethical theory between the Kantian concerns with freedom and duty with which, as a Lutheran, she had been raised, and Aristotelian concerns with the flourishing of character to which she was increasingly attracted. Sometimes she seemed almost to apply a Kantian severity to issues of character, as if presuming that qualities of character ought to be in a person's own immediate control. But such tendencies were tempered by an unusually compassionate understanding of how habits and character need to develop over time. In the end, Aristotle won over Kant, and this goes some way, I believe, towards explaining her interest in the Aristotelian views she defended in her dissertation, reproduced here.

In the pages that follow, Eunice is concerned with the problem of "akrasia," or, in its tendentious English translation, "weakness of will" (the Greek is ũed in order to be more neutral about the diagnosis of the difficulty). The problem is this: it would seem a truism that people sometimes act in ways other than they think best. Despite full knowledge of the unwanted consequences, smokers smoke, dieters ignore their diet, and writers up against a deadline spend a day at the beach. On the other hand, there is another truism, a basic principle of practical rationality that seems everywhere employed in the explanation of intentional action: people (try to) do what they believe will best secure what they most prefer. Versions of this principle are presupposed by Socrates and Plato, articulated as the "practical syllogism" in Aristotle, and play a central role in modern decision theory as the principle of "the maximization of expected utility." For many, it can seem to be partly constitutive of the very concept of intentional action. But if some form of this principle is true, how could cases of akrasia possibly occur? Acting for a lesser preference, whether a pleasure, a habit, a momentary craving, would seem to be ruled out as not only irrational, but psychologically inexplicable: an akrates would seem to be like someone choosing an apple rather than an orange, even though she really preferred the orange. Evidently, one of the truisms must not be true—or someone has to do a good deal of explaining.

Eunice considers three responses to these problems: there are those who hold to both truisms, people she calls "Believers" in akrasia who try to explain it by practical reason by invoking some distinction between various attitudes (e.g., thinking vs. willing) that might end the apparent conflict; then there are the Believers like Donald Davidson (1969),* who are prepared to abandon the truism about practical reason at least in explaining akrasia, finding the phenomenon in its purest form "essentially surd." Finally there are the "Skeptics," like Socrates, Plato, and Aristotle, who deny our first truism, claiming that genuine cases of akrasia couldn't possibly occur. This last has seemed to many people the most desperate of the responses, preserving the principle of practical reason merely by denying the evident data.

Nevertheless, it is this latter Skeptical alternative that Eunice defends. She first examines a theory that permits the first sort of response, Alvin Goldman's (1970) theory that action is determined not by what agents *think best*, but by what they *desire most*. She argues that such "strength of desire" accounts render the principle of practical reason vacuous or false: either we suppose that the winning desire was "stronger" merely because it is the one that did in fact win out, in which case the principle is circular; or we rely on the only independent evidence we have for identifying the strongest desire, the avowed preferences of the agent, in which case, incidents of akrasia show the principle to be false. She then turns to Davidson's view, finding it problematic in a number of ways, not least in failing to provide an adequate account of akrasia: it can't distinguish the akrates from someone who merely acts, entirely inexplicably, on a lesser preference. This failure, she argues, conflicts with the claim, otherwise accepted by Davidson, that akratic acts are fully intentional.

---

*References are to materials listed in the selected bibliography at the end of the dissertation. Those that occur only in the introduction will be found in the updated addendum to that bibliography on p. 237.

The version of the Skeptical response that Eunice defends is that presented by Aristotle in Chapter VII of his *Nichomachian Ethics*. Aristotle claims there that akrasia involves a very specific kind of cognitive breakdown: a crucial bit of the agent's knowledge of the particulars of her situation is momentarily forgotten; it becomes merely "potential knowledge," like the temporarily suspended knowledge of someone mad, asleep, or drunk. Eunice locates this account not in a causal but rather in a general "teleological theory" of human action, of the sort that was advanced some years ago by Charles Taylor (1964) and G.H. von Wright (1971), arguing that, so located, it can deal with a number of objections that have been lodged against it. Throughout the discussion, she employs a rich variety of examples, both of her own and from Dostoyevsky, Thomas Mann, Doris Lessing, in an effort to show how attention to the details of purported cases of akrasia ought to give us pause in taking common descriptions of them at face value. The re-descriptions recommended by Aristotle's theory may not do as much violence to ordinary intuitions as one might initially suppose; at any rate, she argues, they do far less violence than that done by the claims of the Believers. In making these latter comparisons, Eunice nicely begins to raise some general methodological issues about the role of theory in guiding our purportedly pre-theoretic intuitions about the "data" of human action, and about how those intuitions can therefore not be expected to play the decisive role philosophers often presume them to play. In these ways her work is of interest not only as a piece of classical scholarship, action theory, and moral psychology, but as a piece of meta-philosophy, philosophy about the methodology of philosophical disputes. Recognizing these contributions, the Harvard philosophy department awarded Eunice the prize for the best dissertation of 1976.

After finishing this work, Eunice went on to try to apply her Aristotelian model to actual struggles people have with keeping to their resolves. She investigated ways in which the idea of "potential knowledge" provided a way of understanding some of the techniques that have been developed for overcoming (what people have taken to be) recurrent akrasia, particularly in the cases of diets and smoking. That discussion displays the same fine feel for the nuances of mind and action that characterizes the dissertation. Unfortunately, she did not live to complete this further work.

The problem of akrasia continues to be the object of much philosophical dispute. Bogen and Moravcsik (1982) and Dahl (1984) interpret and defend Aristotle's view in ways very different from Eunice's (and from each other's), and the Believer's position has been developed in a number of ways that may not be susceptible to her criticisms: Watson (1977), for example, expands on Santas' (1971) distinction between "evaluational" and "motivational" desires, and Cohen (1986) and Rey (1988) try to distinguish what an agent genuinely believes and desires from what she merely avows. Rich discussions of other details of akrasia may be found in Rorty (1980, 1981), Stocker (1984), and Mele (1987); of issues surrounding "strength of desire" in Bach (1984), and of alternatives to maximization in practical reason in Slote (1989). As Eunice would have been the first to recognize, her work is thus by no means the last word on this vexing problem, but it is a useful and eloquent one—forceful, subtle, imaginative—deserving the attention of Aristotle scholars and philosophers of mind and action alike.

*—Georges Rey*
*University of Maryland at College Park*
*15 November 1989*

# Addendum to Selected Bibliography (November 1989)

Bach, K., "Default Reasoning: Jumping to Conclusions and Knowing When to Think Twice," *Pacific Philosophical Quarterly*, 65 (1984): 37–58.

Bogen, J., and J. Moravcsik, "Aristotle's Forbidden Sweets," *Journal of the History of Philosophy*, April 1982: 11–129.

Cohen, S., "The Problem of the Problem of Akrasia," *Pacific Philosophical Quarterly*, 67 (January 1986).62–72.

Dahl, N., *Practical Reason, Aristotle, and Weakness of the Will*, Minneapolis: University of Minnesota Press, 1984.

Mele, A., *Irrationality: An Essay on Akrasia, Self-Deception, and Self-Control.*, New York: Oxford University Press, 1987.

Rey, G., "Towards a Computational Theory of Akrasia and Self-Deception," in Maclaughlin, B. and A. Rorty, *Perspectives on Self Deception*: 264–96.

Rorty, A., "Where Does the Akratic Break Take Place?," in *Mind in Action*, Boston: Beacon Press 1988: 229–45 (originally published 1980).

Rorty, A., "Akrasia and Conflict," in *Mind in Action*, Boston: Beacon Press, 1988: 246–70 (originally published 1981).

Slote, M., *Beyond Optimizing: A Study of Rational Choice*, Cambridge: Harvard University Press, 1989.

Stocker, M., "Some Structures for Akrasia," *History of Philosophy Quarterly*, 1 (July 1984): 267–80.

Watson, G., "Skepticism About Weakness of Will," *Philosophical Review*, 86: 316–39.

ACKNOWLEDGMENTS

This thesis is the result of a practical as well as a theoretical interest in the regrettably familiar phenomenon of akrasia, otherwise known as knowing the better and doing the worse. I would like to thank friends and colleagues (indeed, even strangers) for generously contributing first-person data, as well as theoretical speculations thereupon. The completion of this piece is perhaps some evidence that explanation and understanding, even outside the physical sciences, can be an aid to control of the phenomenon explained and understood.

But more particular thanks are in order. To Frederick Stoutland, who first introduced me to the pleasures and power of philosophical thought. To John Cooper and G.E.L. Owen, for their guidance to the philosophical excitement to be gained from the Greek philosophers. To the Society for Women in Philosophy, for sustaining that pleasure and excitement. To my committee, Robert Nozick and Terry Irwin, no less for their encouragement than for the prompt, meticulous, and helpful criticism of early drafts and yet more embryonic notions. But my warmest and widest gratitude goes to my dear friend Georges Rey. In his indefatigable enthusiasm for philosophy he has taught me many things; his patience in discussing akrasia has improved this thesis immeasurably.

CONTENTS

ACKNOWLEDGMENTS . . . . . . . . . . . . . . . . . . . . . . . . i

CHAPTER I.   IS THERE A PROBLEM ABOUT AKRASIA? . . . . . . . . .   1

    A. The Intuitive Problem . . . . . . . . . . . . . . .   2
    B. Akrasia Defined . . . . . . . . . . . . . . . . . .  13
    C. The Definition Refined . . . . . . . . . . . . . .  24
        1. Akrasia as intentional . . . . . . . . . . .  25
        2. Open to the akrates to do better . . . . . .  31
        3. Practical judgment . . . . . . . . . . . . .  31
    D. The Project from Here . . . . . . . . . . . . . .  34

CHAPTER II.  MISTAKING THE WANTON FOR THE AKRATES . . . . . . .  42

    A. Motivations to Want Theories . . . . . . . . . . .  44
    B. Goldman's *Theory of Human Action*: The Best Extant
       Account . . . . . . . . . . . . . . . . . . . . .  52
        1. Wants . . . . . . . . . . . . . . . . . . .  53
        2. Wants and explanations . . . . . . . . . . .  58
        3. Want explanations and akrasia . . . . . . .  71
    C. Scylla and Charybdis: Falseness or Vacuity . . . .  74
        1. The account of akrasia . . . . . . . . . . .  75
        2. The general theory . . . . . . . . . . . . .  84

CHAPTER III. THE DAVIDSONIAN AKRATES . . . . . . . . . . . . .  91

    A. The Intuitive Problem . . . . . . . . . . . . . .  92
    B. The Solution: The Weatherman Approach . . . . . . 102
        1. Picture of practical reason . . . . . . . . 102
        2. Solution to the problem of akrasia . . . . . 111
    C. Criticism of the Solution . . . . . . . . . . . . 113
    D. The Weatherman Approach in Perspective . . . . . 129
        1. Token materialism and the anomaly of the
           mental . . . . . . . . . . . . . . . . . . 133
        2. Criticism of the perspective . . . . . . . . 135
    E. Summary So Far . . . . . . . . . . . . . . . . . 140

CHAPTER IV.  TELEOLOGICAL EXPLANATION . . . . . . . . . . . . 145

    A. Back to the Data . . . . . . . . . . . . . . . . 145
    B. Final Causes . . . . . . . . . . . . . . . . . . 152
    C. Final Causes and Akrasia . . . . . . . . . . . . 165

CHAPTER V.   THE ARISTOTELIAN AKRATES . . . . . . . . . . .   184

    A.  Analysis of <u>Nicomachean</u> <u>Ethics</u> VII, 1-3 . . .   185
        1.  Preparatory moves . . . . . . . . . . .   185
        2.  Aristotle's account . . . . . . . . . .   189
    B.  <u>Nicomachean</u> <u>Ethics</u> VII in Perspective  . . . .   205
        1.  Aristotle and final causes    . . . . . .   206
        2.  The place of potential knowledge  . . .   211
        3.  Theoretical elegance . . . . . . . . . .   215
    C.  Concluding Remarks . . . . . . . . . . . . .   221
        1.  Defense against objections . . . . . . .   222
        2.  In retrospect ... . . . . . . . . . . .   230

SELECTED BIBLIOGRAPHY . . . . . . . . . . . .  . . . .  . . . .   233

CHAPTER I

IS THERE A PROBLEM ABOUT AKRASIA?

Persons, patently, do not always behave reasonably. They act thoughtlessly, impulsively, carelessly. They act with lack of foresight, insight, attention, imagination. Through these and other failures, they harm their own interests unwittingly. Through these and other failures, they unwittingly harm the interests of other persons whom they do not want to harm. Persons also, it seems, harm themselves and others wittingly. They are, on occasion, 'swept away' by lust, jealousy, or rage. Though they know the harm that they intend to do, they 'cannot restrain themselves'. In such a case, we are inclined to say, they 'could not help it'.

Persons also, it seems, wittingly harm their own, or others, interests, even though they do not want to do so, and even though they could have avoided doing so. Such is the stuff of akrasia.

While unhappy facts, no doubt, from a practical point of view, cases of unwitting unreasonableness have not seemed conceptually problematic, in any serious way, even to philosophers. They are full of philosophical interest, certainly, but no one has ever questioned the possibility of their very occurrence; no one has ever suggested that there is something seriously wrong, even incoherent, about this way of describing them. Cases of so-called 'psychological compulsion' are unhappier yet, from a practical point of view. The consequences are often more dire; important aspects of the 'personhood' of the agent may even be called into question. But again, there is no controversy about the existence of cases such as these, or about the coherence of describing some behavior in this way.

Akratic acts, by contrast, have seemed to some--philosophers and others--to pose acute conceptual difficulties, in addition to the obvious practical ones. There seems to be a special difficulty in explaining such actions. The very facts which do explain, for example, an unwittingly cruel remark (thoughtlessness, lack of insight, etc.) here do not obtain; and, ex hypothesi, the akrates could have done otherwise. Some philosophers have argued that akrasia, as ordinarily understood, is quite impossible to explain; the admission of such a phenomenon would contradict general principles of action explanation. It is for this reason that they have been tempted to deny its very existence. Let us focus the problem more clearly.

A. The Intuitive Problem

There seem to be occasions on which a person performs an action which, all things considered, she/he knows, or judges, it would be better for her/him not to perform. Nonetheless she/he has a reason for the action, and performs it for that reason. This is the (ostensible) phenomenon of akrasia. There is a problem about akrasia because its existence is not easily reconcilable with beliefs we hold about intentional action which seem obviously true. It seems that when a person acts intentionally she/he acts 'in the light of some imagined good' (Aquinas).

That is, there are aims or goals she/he wishes to realize; some of them can be realized through actions she/he is in a position to perform; and she/he acts, intentionally, in order to realize states of affairs which she/he considers desirable or good. There is a *prima facie* contradiction between such a view of intentional action and the foregoing description of akrasia, for akrasia is precisely intentional action which the agent judges to be contrary to her/his good.

Consider the following case: "I want a pin" says John. "For my collection" he explains. But searching for another pin now will make him miss the plane for Paris. "I grant that," says John. "All things considered I certainly ought not to pause just now to collect another pin. Indeed, the hobby itself is beginning to bore me. Still, adding to my collection possesses some, if little, value." And so he searches, collects one more pin, and misses the plane to Paris.

Surely we would find such a person odd. Surely we would insist that his account of his action simply won't do. We might well suspect that he wants to miss that plane, but won't tell us why. Or we might suspect that the pin collection is not what it appears. Do the pins contain microfilms? Has a crucial message been lost? Normally, that a person has *a* reason to perform an action, if she/he simultaneously has an overriding reason to refrain, is not a sufficient explanation of her/his performance of that action. We expect that, for a person's acting on a reason to be explanatory it must be the reason the person considers best in the circumstances. Hence our positing of another reason altogether than the one that John has offered us.

Now the explanation offered by John is <u>logically indistinguishable</u> from the explanations characteristically offered by the akrates. I smoke for the pleasure, although I judge that pleasure to be not worth it; I languished in bed to avoid the pressures of the day, though I realized that the pressures would be greater yet after the wasted morning; I boarded the airplane because it would have been awkward to refuse, though of course social awkwardness is nothing compared to risking a crash. While each of these reasons surely provides <u>a</u> reason for the act performed, it just as surely provides no more than that. A part of the puzzle about akrasia is that we are inclined, at least at first, to accept any explanation of just this form. When offered the logically parallel explanation by John, we rejected it straightaway.

Let us call those who reject such explanations from the akrates, as well as from John, 'skeptics' with respect to the existence of open-eyed akrasia. The skeptic argues that akrasia, as described above, contradicts certain general truths about human action; consequently this description cannot be correct. The skeptic thus denies the possibility of this seemingly familiar phenomena. Let us call those concerned to salvage the possibility of the phenomena 'believers' with respect to open-eyed akrasia. The believers argue that the explanation offered by the akrates, suitably interpreted, can be distinguished from that offered by John. Suitably interpreted, open-eyed akrasia is compatible with reasonable general beliefs about action.

Socrates is surely the most famous of the skeptics. He claimed that it is quite impossible to explain any case of open-eyed akrasia.

Indeed, he argued that we may shortly be reduced to incoherence if we even try. Thus, he denied its existence. In the *Protagoras* he indicates that many would disagree:

> Most men . . . maintain that there are many who recognize the best but are unwilling to act on it. It may be open to them, but they do otherwise. Whenever I ask what is the reason for this, they answer that those who act in this way are overcome by pleasure or pain. (352d-e)

He then considers their claim in the light of the hedonist thesis-- "Then your idea of evil is pain, and of good is pleasure" (354c). Next he performs a deft and elegant *reductio* on the common belief. If the good is pleasure, and pleasure the good, then those who fail to do what is best, knowingly, would be in the position of those who fail to do the pleasurable because, according to this account, they are "overcome by pleasure". But by substitutivity of identity:

> I fear that if our questioner is ill-mannered he will laugh and retort: 'What ridiculous nonsense, for a man to do evil, knowing it is evil and that he ought not to do it, because he is overcome by good. (355c)

Thus:

> . . . no one who either knows or believes that there is another possible course of action better than the one he is following, will ever continue on his present course when he might choose the better. (358c)

The success of this *reductio* does not depend on the hedonist assumption; it works just as well if we substitute 'honor', 'wealth', or even 'virtue' for 'pleasure'.[1] Indeed, it does not depend on **any** particular account of what makes the better better. The mere capacity for

---

[1] Gerasimos Santas, "Plato's Protagoras and the Explanation of Weakness," *The Philosophical Review*, LXXV (1966).

comparative judgments of relative value is all that is required. Donald Davidson generates a similar Socratic quandary about akrasia using no particular account of value at all.[1]

Davidson suggests that the admission of open-eyed akrasia contradicts certain general beliefs about human action that "have the air of self-evidence". The problem posed by this (apparent) contradiction is, he says, "acute enough to be called a paradox." Davidson formalizes these general beliefs in two principles:[2]

P1. If an agent wants to do x more than he wants to do y and believes himself free to do either x or y , then he will intentionally do x if he does either x or y intentionally.

P2. If an agent judges that it would be better to do x than to do y, then he wants to do x more than he wants to do y.

P1 and P2 together entail that if an agent judges that it would be better for her/him to do x than to do y, and believes her/himself free to do either x or y, than she/he will do x if she/he does either x or y intentionally. An akratic act, however, would be an instance of y, not x. Thus, if these principles are true, it would seem to show that it is false that there are akratic acts.

It is not, however, _simply_ false that there are akratic acts; no skeptic _simply_ denies the occurrence of acts that others assert to have occurred. It is not the events _per se_, but rather the appropriate descriptions of these events that is at issue. There are two

---

[1] Donald Davidson, "How is Weakness of Will Possible?", in Moral Concepts, ed. Joel Feinberg (London: Oxford University Press, 1970), pp.93-113.

[2] Ibid., pp.94-5.

routes commonly taken by those who, in company with Socrates and Davidson, sense a contradiction here. One is the Socratic route, of assimilating ostensible cases of open-eyed akrasia to one or another form of unwitting unreasonableness. The other, more common, is to assimilate akrasia to one or another form of psychological compulsion.

Thus, Socrates:

> That which the many describe as enslavement to oneself is nothing but ignorance and mastery of oneself is nothing but wisdom . . . and we define ignorance as having a false belief and being mistaken. (<u>Protagoras</u>, 358c)

Aristotle refines the relevant sense of 'ignorance'; Davidson proliferates the relevant sorts of 'judgment' involved.

Plato, in the <u>Timaeus</u>, favors the compulsion line:

> . . . in general, all that which is termed incontinence of pleasure and is deemed a reproach under the idea that the wicked voluntarily do wrong is not justly a matter of reproach. For no man is voluntarily bad, but the bad become bad by reason of an ill-disposition of the body and bad education--things which are hateful to every man and happen to him against his will. (86d-e)

Hare, following Plato, makes psychological inability the paradigm case of akrasia.[1] This is surely the most plausible account of the (all too) familiar plights of Medea and St. Paul. Indeed, in these cases, the compulsion seems even to stem from sources other than the agent's own psyche. "Some God is on its [desire's] side" cries Medea; Paul, less graphically, pleads, "If what I do is against my will, clearly it is no longer I who am the agent, but sin that lodges in me." (Romans 7) Less worn, and more poignant, is Thomas Mann's brilliant figure, Praisegod Piepsum. Here, surely, is a 'weakness' which is stronger than its

---

[1] R. M. Hare, <u>Freedom and Reason</u> (Oxford: Clarendon Press, 1963), p.71

possessor, if ever there was one.

> In the first place, he drank . . . . Once he had been able to resist, to some extent, though yielding to it by bouts. But when his wife and child were snatched from him, when he had no work and no position, nothing to support him, when he stood alone on this earth, then his weakness took more and more the upper hand. . . . . He drank because he had no self-respect, and he had no self-respect because the continual breakdown of his good intentions ate it away. At home in his wardrobe he kept a bottle with a poisonous-colored liquor in it, the name of which I will refrain from mentioning. Before this wardrobe Praisegod Piepsam had before now gone literally on his knees, and in his wrestlings had bitten his tongue--and still in the end capitulated. I do not like even to mention such things--but after all they are very instructive.[1]

There need be no quarrel amongst the skeptics as to whether akrasia is 'really' a kind of unwitting unreasonableness, or is 'really' a kind of psychological inability. It might well be that some cases of ostensible akrasia are one while others are the other. Further argument here would, in any case, be short-sighted. The skeptics agree on a matter which is far more fundamental; it is, in addition, strongly counter-intuitive. That is, all skeptics insist that _every_ case of (ostensible) akrasia _must_ be assimilated to one or another of these _other_ sorts of unreason. Our original intuitions, of course, suggest that there _is also_ a separate type of unreasonable action--akrasia proper--which is quite distinct from any of these other cases. It is this intuition that the believers are concerned to salvage.

The believers are those who are inclined to insist that there is such a thing as akrasia proper, in addition to whatever other varieties of unreasonable action. The most fundamental disagreement regarding

---

[1] Thomas Mann, "The Way to the Churchyard," in _Stories of Three Decades_, transl. H. T. Lowe-porter (New York: Alfred Knopf, 1936), p. 80.

akrasia, then, may be expressed as follows:

> Does it never happen that I have an unclouded, unwavering judgement that my act is not for the best, and yet perform it . . . with no hint of compulsion or the compulsive?[1]

The skeptics answer "Never"; the believers, "Sometimes".

Most of us seem to be believers, at least in a part of our intuitions. We do seem to believe that there is such a thing as akrasia proper. And we are inclined to accept explanations which mention patently insufficient reasons in this special case--although not in other cases, such as that of John, the pin collector. Our intuitions here have philosophical support. Disagreement with Socrates is a far more prevalent philosophical view than is any form of agreement. According to these philosophers, our intuitive characterization of akrasia proper is indeed accurate. Each clause is necessary to capture the real nature of the phenomenon. And, they argue, general truths about action can accommodate this kind of case.

Thus, many philosophers have attempted to provide an account of open-eyed akrasia. The various explanations offered, however, do not coincide; many are not even compatible. There is no clear consensus amongst anti-Socratic philosophers as to how open-eyed akrasia _is_ to be explained. Thus despite strong resistance to Socrates, the current state of philosophical thought about akrasia is one of conflict, complexity, and confusion.

I believe that the mere fact of this situation is instructive. Philosophical thought about akrasia to date has not appreciated the

---

[1]Davidson, "How is Weakness of Will Possible?", p.100.

theoretical sources of Socratic skepticism. Because these sources have been unnoticed they have not been addressed. But an adequate account of open-eyed akrasia--if one is possible--must address the sources of this skepticism. This is because skeptical intuitions about akrasia are no less fundamental than are believer intuitions. They are simply less often noticed. An adequate account of open-eyed akrasia--if one is to be possible-- must include an account of the fact that our intuitions about the possibility, or impossibility, of open-eyed akrasia are **strongly** **ambivalent**. The near-universal *first* reaction to Davidson's question is to strongly agree with the believers. However, upon reflection, or when pressed about related matters, there is also a near-universal, but less often noticed, tendency to **redescribe** the particular case at hand, in company with the skeptics. Sometimes the case is redescribed along Socratic lines; sometimes along compulsion lines; perhaps most often the case is redescribed by invoking some sort of unconscious motivation. When this last strategy is employed, the act is attributed to **another** **reason** **altogether** than the akratic reason, recognized to be inadequate. This last strategy is no less Socratic in essence than the other two.

A clear illustration of this strong ambivalence in our intuitions is to be found in Dostoyevsky's Underground Man. He begins, in company with the believers, by attacking Socrates directly.

> Tell me, who was it first declared, proclaiming it to the whole world, that a man does evil only because he does not know his real interests, and if he is enlightened and has his eyes opened to his own best and normal interests, man will cease to do evil and at once become virtuous and noble . . . since it is well known that no man can knowingly act against his best interests, consequently he will inevitably, so to speak, begin to do good.

Oh what a baby! Oh, what a pure innocent child! What about all those millions of incidents testifying to the fact that men have knowingly, that is in full understanding of their own best interests, put them in the background and taken a perilous and uncertain course not because anybody or anything drove them to it, but solely and simply because they did not choose to follow the appointed road.[1]

From this, and similar, passages the Underground Man is commonly taken to be Socrates' most vociferous opponent. Moreover, he appears to be an intelligent opponent--pointing to 'empirical evidence' to counter Socrates' purely logical moves about an empirical phenomenon. But ambivalence appears at once. His barb seems clearly aimed at Socrates' account of akrasia, but it just as clearly misses that particular mark, with his very next breath.[2]

What, in fact, do these 'millions of incidents' show, according to the Underground Man? They show, he says, that "obstinacy and self-will meant more to them than any kind of advantage." It is not (really) Socrates' views on akrasia at all that prompts his railings; rather it is the omission from the standard lists of goods and interests of that "primary best good which is dearer to him than all else." It is the failure of some to realize that one may be rational in wanting what is thought not to be 'sensible' to which he objects. "One's own free and unfettered volition, one's own caprice, however wild, one's own fancy, inflamed sometimes to the point of madness--that is the one

---

[1] Dostoyevsky, Notes from Underground, trans. Jesse Coulson (London: Penguin Classics, 1972), p. 29.

[2] It hits instead--or nearly hits--the quite separate Socratic doctrine that a life of (Greek) virtue is the best life for a person.

best and greatest good." The rational, indeed the noble, person on this view is one who "is willing to jeopardize his very gingerbread . . . just so he can assert that people are still people and not piano keys."

Thus, it is not akrasia at all about which Dostoyevsky is rhapsodizing. He is not <u>even talking about</u> action contrary to what a person judges to be better for her/him. Rather, he is praising a certain (intemperate, to be sure) conception of <u>what is in fact better</u> for persons--for beings having volition, passion, and fancy, as well as the ability 'to extract square roots'.[1]

This Socratic twist from even the Underground Man is in fact characteristic of the discussions of many non-philosophers, which are taken to be discussions of akrasia proper. We begin, in a non-Socratic fashion, discussing an apparent case of clear-headed unreasonable action; but Socratic intuitions subtly insinuate themselves, and we end up with an account of quite a different phenomenon--ranging from a new account of what's thought best (Dostoyevsky, Lessing below); some version of psychological compulsion (Medea, St. Paul, Praisegod Piepsum); or the akrates is turned into one or another of the unwitting varieties of unreasonable person (e.g. one engaged in self-deception, hypocrisy, <u>mauvais foi</u>, one who forgot, didn't realize, and the rest.)

Thus, both the believers and the skeptics find a response in a part of our deeply entrenched intuitions. On the one hand, open-eyed

---

[1] Dostoyevsky, <u>Notes</u>, pp. 31, 36, 33, 38.

akrasia certainly seems to exist. On the other hand, we display a strong tendency to redescribe any particular case, in company with the skeptics. Open-eyed akrasia, it seems, is not easily accommodated with other general beliefs we hold about action. The various ways in which we seek to make it compatible testify to the strength and tenacity of intentional explanation.

My aim in this thesis is to resolve this ambivalence, to the degree that is possible. I shall investigate the theoretical underpinnings of the claims of each side, with a view to determining which side is backed by the stronger arguments. I assume that a necessary condition of granting the possibility of open-eyed akrasia is that we produce a coherent, preferably plausible, account of it. One prime condition of adequacy on such an account is that it be compatible with a good general theory of action. In the event that such an account is not to be found, our best strategy would be three-fold: to evaluate the theoretical sources of the skeptics' skepticism; to see how well they can reply to the most strenuous objections of the believers; and finally, to see how well they can account for the believers' side of our intuitions.

## B. Akrasia Defined

Our project, then, is to find out whether open-eyed akrasia is possible; that is, to determine whether it can be accounted for.. If it *is not* possible, so described, we need to produce an account which is theoretically defensible. Clearly, in order to do justice to the dispute between the skeptics and believers in open-eyed akrasia we need to focus on the theoretically most difficult case. In order to refute the skeptic we would need to produce an account of this class, else we would "show a certain weakness as philosophers" by knocking down straw men, and leaving the central issue untouched.

In this section, and the next, I shall characterize what I take to be the theoretically most difficult class of akratic acts. It is this class that the believers must account for in order to make good their view, in order to justify the claim that open-eyed akrasia is in fact possible. At least these conditions (and perhaps others as well) are necessary if we are to address, rather than avoid the central issue.

I shall adopt the definition of akrasia proposed by Davidson[1] (clauses a)-c)), with one minor modification (clause d)):

> D: In doing x an agent acts akratically if and only if a) the agent does x intentionally; b) the agent believes that there is an alternative action y open to her/him; c) the agent judges that, all things considered, it would be better to do y than to do x; and d) the agent regrets having performed the action.

The crux of the dispute between the believers and the skeptics is this: is the occurrence of acts satisfying D compatible with good general principles of action explanation, or are such acts ruled out by these principles?

This definition deviates somewhat from traditional conceptions of akrasia in ways that are important for my purposes. I wish to consider all and only those cases where we are not straightaway inclined to assimilate akrasia (that is, akrasia proper) to some other variety of unreasonable

---

[1] Davidson, "How is Weakness of Will Possible?", p.94

action; we shall be concerned only with those cases where our ambivalence about the possibility of such action is not easily resolved. The class of actions that I shall consider akratic, and with whose explanation I shall be concerned, is broader, along one parameter, narrower, along another, than the traditional class. My definition is to be preferred to any proposed alternative in that it best approximates our pre-theoretic intuitions. More precisely: a) it captures all those plausible cases included on any definition; b) it captures further plausible cases, which are excluded from the traditional class; c) it excludes certain implausible cases which would be allowed by the alternatives.

Traditional discussions of akrasia, from Plato and Aristotle on, have tended to focus on cases where <u>desire</u> distracts us from the <u>good</u>, or forces us bad; or cases where we follow a "beastly selfish <u>passion</u> over the call of <u>duty</u> and morality."[1] Let us call such cases the 'traditional class' of akratic acts. The class of acts captured by my definition D deviates from the traditional class in the following significant respects.

According to D, an akratic act need not (although it may) have anything to do with following passion at the expense of obligation, morality, or prudence. It need not (although it may) have anything to do with electing 'the pleasant' at the expense of 'the good'. My definition is pointedly non-committal on these matters; I do not want to rule out all such cases, but I certainly do not want to make them central. The reason for neutrality here is two-fold.

---

[1] Davidson, "How is Weakness of Will Possible?", p. 101.

First, many members of the traditional class are easily, and correctly, assimilated to some other variety of unreasonable action. Thus, they are not, pre-theoretically, good candidates for open-eyed 'akrasia proper'. An account of them would therefore not be an account of the theoretically hardest case. Cases that satisfy D, by contrast, do seem to be the sort we need to account for, if one is to reply to Socrates and the skeptics. Secondly, there are many pre-theoretically interesting cases of akrasia, captured by D, which would be simply excluded from the traditional class. Thus an account of that class, even were it adequate for those cases, would still be incomplete as an account of akrasia proper. Let me illustrate each of these points.

The class of acts captured by D is narrower than the traditional class in that it excludes certain cases which are clearly not central cases of akrasia. The context of strong desires, or 'beastly passions' is often a context where we are inclined to say that the agent 'could not help' doing what she/he did. Such an assimilation of akrasia to cases of 'psychological compulsion' is precisely what the believers in open-eyed akrasia are concerned to avoid. Thus, it is only reasonable to begin with cases which are clearly not cases of psychological compulsion. Of course, any case of desire or passion where the person could have done otherwise is allowed according to D.

Secondly, the 'good' has some, 'prudence' and 'obligation' even more, associations with practical principles which represent the dictates of god, government, or peer group. These may or may not coincide with the agent's own practical principles. (It was such associations which led the Underground Man to think, falsely, that he disagreed with Socrates on akrasia.) It may, on occasion, take strength of character to follow one's own lights, against prevailing standards, but it is not conceptually problemmatic if one does. Indeed, I do not find anything outré about a person, on principle, sacrificing prudence to impulse. (If you do, well and good; such cases are not ruled out either.) The class of actions that is central to akrasia is only that involving action against the agent's own judgement of what it would be better to do, which may or may not include being better for the agent's health, wealth, security, family, friends, or country.

The class of acts captured by D includes a wide variety of pre-theoretically interesting cases of akrasia which are excluded from the traditional class. In this important respect, my class of akratic acts is broader (and thus more comprehensive) than the traditional class. Aside from the intrinsic interest of these cases, it is this broader class for which we would need to account in order to answer the skeptic.

Consider first the well-worn examples of 'human weaknesses' invariably trotted out in discussions of akrasia: the fat man indulging in a hot fudge sundae; the (unhappily) enlightened smoker, who knows all the statistics about lung cancer, emphysema, heart disease, but lights another; the lay-about still languishing in bed at noon. There is no denying that such activities can be pleasurable. Still, it is no less clear that many with a 'weakness' for such delights do not take pleasure in a good number of their indulgences. Rather, the 'weakness' persists, the indulgence continues, despite nausea from too many sundaes, sharp lung stabs from too many cigarettes, dull sluggishness from too much sleep. At least not all such cases need involve pleasure. Nor is it plausible to believe that the akrates, who has come to such a pass, thinks there is pleasure to be had. Thus, the reason for which she/he acts must be <u>other</u> than pleasure. These cases would therefore be excluded from the traditional class; but they surely want explaining.

The traditional class makes more serious omissions. Even for the eaters, smokers, and sleepers who are not positively suffering from a surfeit of 'pleasures', there are, more often than not, reasons other than pleasure which it is plausible to think motivate the activity. (Or, at least, reasons in addition to pleasure, when the motivation is complex.) For those akrateis with a touch of psychological theory, and a modicum of self-knowledge, they know it. Eating is not only a sensuous pleasure, it is also the most primitive of gratifications. The akrates with respect to food is often regressing as well as feasting. Smoking is a sensuous pleasure. But Madison Avenue has also firmly linked it, in the western psyche, with a wordly elan and sex appeal. It is doubtful that many persons would <u>acquire</u> the capacity to take pleasure in smoking were it not for these induced motivations. Again, behaviour motivated in these ways would be excluded from the traditional class. But we surely want an account of them.

More strikingly, there are clearly cases of acting against one's better judgement where the claims of pleasure are, akratically, not attended to. Davidson has reminded us of their importance. They are captured by my definition, but would be excluded from the traditional class. Consider an example.

Prior to 1970 the terms of the NDEA loan program were such that it provided a good investment opportunity for most graduate students, as well as funding for bare survival. A loan accumulated no interest until completion of the degree; after that the rate was a mere 3%, well below the level of inflation. More importantly, up to half the loan would be cancelled should the student teach for five years, something most students intended to do anyway. A reasonable student might have reasoned thus: Going into (unnecessary) debt is in general to be avoided. It is onerous to sacrifice today for pleasures already past. Moreover it's risky; who knows what the future will bring. On the other hand, I can make a rough but reasonable calculus of diminishing marginal utility. The negative value of repayment then is <u>much</u> less than the positive value of the money to me now. All things considered, I ought to take out a healthy loan. But the student does not take out the loan. She/he is akratic with respect to applying for a loan. She/he akratically sacrifices the claims of present pleasure to a believed irrational aversion to indebtedness.

Finally, there are plenty of cases of acting against one's better judgement where pleasure seems not to be involved at all. These cases are no less puzzling than the foregoing. They are captured by my definition, but would be excluded from the traditional class. An intriguing example of this kind of case is described by Doris Lessing in the <u>Golden Notebook</u>.

An airplane has just failed three times in its attempt to take off from Orley. It taxies back to the building so that mechanics can adjust what they call "a small fault in the engine". They work for awhile; then a loud and animated quarrel breaks out amongst them. The incident is audible and visible to the passengers in the terminal. The waving of arms and shrugging of shoulders subsides into sullenness on the part of the under-mechanics. They drift back to the building.

> The American and Ella exchanged glances. He said, apparently amused: "I don't care much for that", while the voice from the loudspeaker invited them to take their seats. She remarked: "Perhaps we should refuse to go?" He said, showing fine, very white teeth and an enthusiastic beam from boyish blue eyes: "I've got an appointment tomorrow morning." Apparently the appointment was so important it justified the risk of crashing . . . In the brightly lit interior of the aircraft, forty people were in the grip of terror, and concerned with not showing it . . . . [Ella remarks,] "How extraordinary! And every one of these people, with the possible exception of this exhuberant young man, is terrified that the machine is going to crash, and yet we all trooped obediently on to it.[1]

I think one would reasonably balk at calling the whole planeload suicidal. If so, the behaviour of at least some of the passengers is a case of akrasia which is clearly not for pleasure.[2]

Thus, I initially place no fixed restrictions on the reasons which may be akratic reasons, nor on the content or 'objective reasonableness' of the practical judgements acted against. There seem to be akratic acts no less familiar than the traditional ones done 'for pleasure'

---

[1] Doris Lessing, The Golden Notebook, (New York: Ballentine Books, Simon and Schuster, Inc., 1962), pp.316-7. The narrator's own reaction is another instance of the Socratic side of our ambivalent intuitions. She attributes a reason other than the awkwardness of making a scene. She deduces, then calls it a 'discovery' that she must want to die. She speculates on the behaviour of the other passengers: "So perhaps we all feel the same way?"

[2] Cases akin to this are favored examples offered by undergraduate akrates: they drive with reckless, or drunken, drivers, against their better judgement, simply because they feel it would be socially awkward to refuse. There is, certainly, awkwardness and anxiety in the course of action they choose to follow.

against 'the good', done for a wide range of reasons, against a wide range of practical principles. They are no less intuitively puzzling than the traditional cases; perhaps some are more so. We would have shirked an important part of our philosophical task if we did not account for these as well. It will probably be necessary to introduce some restrictions in the end, to rule out certain cases the philosophical imagination has spawned.[1] However, it is important to <u>begin</u> with at least all those cases we find intuitively, psychologically, plausible.

In these important respects my definition of the class of akratic acts agrees with that proposed by Davidson. However, Davidson's definition (clauses a)-c) of $D_1'$ above) unwittingly admits two kinds of cases which are clearly not akrasia, and which generate no intuitive puzzlement. Thus, I have added clause d), "the agent regrets having performed the action", in order to rule out these unwanted cases. The first is a purely formal matter, the second is more substantive.[2]

Probably for every action there is <u>some</u> other action one could perform at that time which would be better. Generally, one does not know <u>what</u> it is/they are, but the barest acquaintance with decision theory teaches one that there is/are <u>some</u> such actions. Clearly no action, of which one judges in this minimal sense only, that it is worse than some alternative is an akratic act. Clause d) rules out this unwanted class

---

[1] Irwin's newspaper chewer, Anscombe's pin collector, and saucer of mud fanatic, Davidson's paint-drinker.

[2] The importance of this clause was pointed out to me by Robert Nozick.

of cases.

More substantively, there is a real and unresolved dispute in moral theory whether the notion of 'good' or the notion of 'right' is the more fundamental. This is the major point at issue between teleological and deontological theorists. Now 'better' (in clause c) of D) is the comparative form of 'good'. However, a Kantian who satisfied conditions a)-c) would surely not be akratic in doing x if x is a case of promise-keeping, and thus her/his duty; or if y is a case of lying, and thus impermissible. For the Kantian, questions of 'right' override questions of 'the good' (and hence 'the better') on principle. Again, clause d) is needed to rule out cases satisfying conditions a)-c) which are clearly not cases of akrasia.

To recapitulate briefly: I have proposed a definition of the theoretically significant class of akratic acts. This definition is to be preferred to any proposed alternative in that it best approximates our pre-theoretic intuition. More precisely: a) it captures all those plausible cases included on any definition; b) it captures further plausible cases, which are excluded from the traditional class; c) it excludes certain implausible cases which are allowed by the alternatives. The most important result of emphasizing these features is that it has brought to the fore the theoretically most difficult cases. It is only by producing an account suitable for these that we will have dealt with the basic point at issue between the Socratic skeptics and the believers in open-eyed akrasia.

My discussion also deviates from a part of the tradition in that its scope is narrower. A few words of explanation are in order.

I shall confine myself to discussion of <u>actions</u> that are akratic, setting aside <u>omissions</u>. That is, I shall not be concerned, in the first instance, with <u>failures</u> to do things that one judges, all things considered, it would be <u>better to have</u> done. I shall discuss only actions of which one judges, all things considered, it would be better <u>not to have</u> done. It may seem that I am thereby setting aside a most common and seductive variety of akrasia. This may well be true.[1]

Still, most of those who believe in open-eyed akrasia believe that there are such actions as well as omissions. This limitation will not affect their general claims substantially. More centrally, it is important to begin with the less complicated task. Omissions are far more difficult than actions to account for philosophically. Consider merely the obscurity of criteria of individuation. Only rarely does any practical principle require one to do a particular kind of action, here, and now; but <u>only</u> such an omission would be strictly parallel to an akratic action. Cases of forebearance are more manageable, but even they are more complex than actions.[2] Have I been akratic if I forbear to apply for the loan today, but do it tomorrow? Probably not. Time enough to account for akratic forbearance when we have a decent account

---

[1] Sidgewick concluded that only omissions in fact present counter-instances to Socrates' doctrine. Henry Sidgewick, "Unreasonable Action," <u>Mind</u>, New Series, Vol. 2 (1893), pp. 174-187.

[2] G.E. M. Anscombe, <u>Intention</u>, (Oxford: Basil Blackwell, 1957), p. 59; Gerog Henrik Von Wright, <u>Explanation and Understanding</u> (Ithaca: Cornell University Press, 1971), pp. 90-91.

of akratic actions.

Secondly, I shall not be concerned, it the first instance, with akrasia as a habit, or a trait of character. This is a more substantive restriction. There are those who think that the explanation of akratic acts is parasitic on the explanation of a weak character. I propose no argument against this view. Aristotle's contrary claim that it is impossible to be habitually akratic (EN 1150b, 1151a) is, at best, counterintuitive. I focus on actions not because I believe that account to be logically prior. It may or may not be. My reasons are purely strategic. Theory of action is, at present, a clearer, more developed field than is the theory of character. Advances in the latter will doubtless cast welcome light on our understanding of akrasia.[1]

### C. The Definition Refined

Several of the terms that figure in D, our definition of akrasia, are theoretically dense. In order to ensure that we focus on the central problem regarding open-eyed akrasia, we need to unpack them. In particular, we need to explicate the relevant sense of an 'intentional act'. Additionally, I shall clarify briefly the sense in which another act is believed by the akrates to be 'open' to her/him, and I shall explicate further the 'judgement' involved. The purpose of these refinements, again, is to articulate the theoretically most difficult case. It is only by producing an account of this central case that Socratic skepticism can be refuted. And, it is primarily by focusing on

---

[1]Forthcoming dissertation by Marcia Homiak, Harvard University.

this central case that the impulse to Socratic skepticism can be adequately understood.

We may comment, in passing, on certain practical difficulties in identifying a nuclear case of akrasia. There may well be disagreement whether one or another of the cases described above is 'really' a case of akrasia. Such disagreement would be uninteresting to pursue. They are cases of akrasia if they satisfy the conditions set out in the definition D; they are not cases of akrasia if they do not. It is not possible to define akrasia ostensively. This is (partly) because there are notorious practical difficulties in showing, of any actual case of unreasonable action, that *it* satisfies any of these conditions, much less all of them together.[1] It is for this reason that I do not propose to 'prove', of any case cited above, that *it* is a nuclear case of akrasia. The skeptic, the believer, and myself, are concerned simply with cases which ex hypothesi do satisfy these conditions.

1. Akrasia as intentional

The notion of intentional action is very complex. We shall consider it again in each of the succeeding chapters. Intuitively, however, few ideas could be more familiar. As Wittgenstein remarked, "Voluntary movement is marked by the absence of surprise." The idea of an action is the idea of what one does. "As physical objects go, my body has an extraordinary repertoire." With it, I can walk, jump, make horses walk

---

[1] See for example Carl G. Hempel, Aspects of Scientific Explanation (New York: The Free Press, 1965), pp. 469-483; D. C. Dennett, "Intentional Systems", Journal of Philosophy, Vol.LXVIII: No.4, Feb. 25, 1971, pp.102-3.

and jump, build bridges, build machines to build bridges, make love and revolutions, betray a trust, save a life. Of particular interest are actions I perform on purpose, for a reason. An intentional action is often defined as an act which an agent does for a reason. To determine what action was performed, we refer to the reason for which it was performed. "An agent performs an intentional act provided there is something he makes happen in the way he intended."[1] There are two aspects of the intentionality of akrasia that are of special importance.

a) 'Strong' intentionality

A part of our entire project will be to set out a correct account of the class of intentional actions in general. But however this may be with the general class, it is with only a part of this class that we shall be primarily concerned. The theoretically central case of akrasia must be an instance of 'strongly intentional' action.

Strongly intentional action is not a sharply delineated class. Rather, it occupies one end of a spectrum, at the other end of which fall many habitual actions (such as Davidsonian toothbrushing most often is), purposeful, yet 'automatic', responses (such as those of a skilled driver on a busy road; a skilled acrobat, diver, or typist exercising her/his skill).

---

[1] Ludwig Wittgenstein, trans. G. E. M. Anscombe, The Philosophical Investigations (Oxford: Basil Blackwell, 1963), #628, p.162; D. G. Brown, Action (London: George Allen and Unwin Ltd., 1968), p.50; Roderick Chisholm, "The Structure of Intention", The Journal of Philosophy, Vol. LXVIII, No.19, (Oct. 8, 1970) p.634.

> The precise force of the expression 'thinking what he was doing' is somewhat elusive. I certainly can run upstairs two at a time from force of habit and at the same time notice that I'm doing so, and even consider how the act is done. I can be a spectator of my habitual and reflex actions and even a diagnostician of them, without these actions ceasing to be automatic . . . Conversely, actions done from motives can be 'naive', i.e. the agent has not coupled and perhaps cannot couple, his action with a secondary operation of telling himself, or others, what he is doing.[1]

Somewhat elusive as this sense is, it is the one I mean to capture. I shall focus on intentional action which an agent does for a reason, and is aware of doing it for that reason.

It is tokens, and not types, of actions which are, or fail to be strongly intentional. If, for example, one brushes ones teeth on Tuesday with (roughly) attention and awareness (as a part, say, of a SmokEnders regime), then on Tuesday the brushing is strongly intentional for the most part, however, the brushing probably is not. Similarly, the very same sort of actions which, for a skilled driver, acrobat, or diver, are normally not strongly intentional, may be so on occasion--when, for example, the expert is teaching that activity to a novice.

b) The akratic reason

An intentional act is one done for a reason. An akratic act is an intentional act done for an akratic reason, simpliciter. The definition of akrasia that I have adopted from Davidson does not specify the description under which the akratic act is intentional. I want to remedy that vagueness here. This is essential if we are to distinguish akrasia

---

[1] Gilbert Ryle, The Concept of Mind, (New York: Barnes and Noble, 1949), p.111.

from two other kinds of cases which also satisfy the vague definition, but are not even irrational.

We surely want to distinguish akrasia from action on a desire which might be called 'coercive'. And we want to distinguish akrasia from action where the real reason, or a part of the real reason, is unconscious.

A coercive desire is a desire to do something which the agent judges to be irrational, or better not to do. Unlike a compulsive desire, it is a desire which can be resisted; an agent can choose to not act on it. Action on such a desire, however, is not akratic; it is not even irrational. Watson has suggested a fruitful definition of a coercive desire:

> A desire may be regarded as coercive if one prefers the pre-desire situation (that is, the present situation minus the desire) to the desire situation, even though, given the desire situation, the perceived alternatives are such that one prefers the satisfaction of the desire to the other options.[1]

Action on a coercive desire is neither akratic nor irrational because, in such a case, the agent judges that the cost of resisting the desire is prohibitive. The agent could resist the desire, but judges that it is not worth it.

The plight of some unhappily enlightened smokers is a good example of action on a coercive desire. It is clear that they are not akratic. Suppose that Jill believes as strongly as she believes anything that she ought to quit smoking. She wishes herself rid of the desire to continue

---

[1]Gary Watson, "The Nature of Responsibility," Unpublished Ph.D. Dissertation, Princeton University, 1972, p.164.

this hazardous, expensive, socially disruptive practice. Then, she calculates the cost of quitting now: she must submit the manuscript soon; attending *also* to the difficulties of quitting would interfere with a single-minded concentration she can ill-afford to lose. It would also, she thinks, make her still more tense. Given these costs, she judges that she had better continue giving in to the desire, at least awhile longer.

Unlike cases of compulsion, this decision may be fully voluntary and responsible. Unlike cases of akrasia, the agent does not act contrary to her/his better judgement. The judgement, in such a case, concerns what it's best to do in circumstances which include both objective facts of the situation *and* the unwanted desire itself. While Jill could resist the desire to smoke, she decides that it is not worth it. Sometimes such a decision is surely rational; more often, no doubt, it is made in bad faith.

Our insistence that the real reason for the act be the akratic reason *simpliciter* rules out such unwanted cases. In the case of Jill, the reason for her smoking is not simply "I want to smoke"; rather it is (something like) "Given that I want to smoke, in these circumstances, the costs of not smoking are too high."

The second class of cases, excluded according to this condition, are cases where the real reason, or a part of the real reason, is unconscious. It is a matter of dispute whether unconsciously motivated actions are correctly called intentional at all.[1] Thus, it is possible

---

[1] Dennett says no; Mullane and Goldman say roughly yes. Dennett,

that such actions are already excluded by the 'intentional' clause. Whatever the correct answer to this turns out to be, such acts are to be excluded from the class of akratic acts. Not all unconsciously motivated acts are even irrational, and their explanation is clearly different from the explanation of akratic acts.

One of the clues by which we are led to look for an unconscious 'real' reason is a case where the proffered reason is not a very good one. Surely this is the case with akratic acts; indeed, it is a part of the definition of akrasia. One natural response of those who reflect on cases of apparent akrasia is precisely to posit an unconscious reason. (c.f. Ella at the airport.) Now, rightly or wrongly[1], post-Freudian common sense feels that an act has been explained when it is shown to contribute to an unconscious goal. Cases of this sort ought to be distinguished from cases in which there is no such goal. It begs the question for the Socratic skeptic to deny any such distinction.

For example, if a case of ostensible akrasia with respect to sweets is truly explained by invoking an unconscious desire to make oneself ugly, lonely and ignored, it would not belong to the class of acts I wish to consider. (Similarly, the Lessing case is not one of akrasia, if Ella is in fact suicidal, as she speculates.) Were one aware of doing it for this reason, it might or might not be a case of akrasia, depending on whether one judged it better not to, all things

---

"Intentional Systems," pp. 174-178; Harvey Mullane, "Psychoanalytic Explanation and Rationality," The Journal of Philosophy, Vol. LXVIII: No. 14, July 22, 1971, pp. 413-426; Alvin Goldman, A Theory of Human Action, (Englewood Cliffs: Prentice-Hall, Inc., 1970), p. 123.

[1] Mullane, "Explanation," p. 24, argues that the appearance of an explanation is misleading.

considered.

Contrary to appearances, it need not be perverse to judge it better to continue indulging, once the 'real reason' has been unearthed. The desire to eat might then be judged coercive, and the costs of resisting it judged prohibitive. Alternatively, one might believe that one would be ugly, lonely, and ignored anyway, even if one were not fat, for independent reasons (e.g. a terrible personality). One might prefer to be disliked for this reason rather than for that.

## 2. 'Open' to the akrates to do otherwise

The second theoretically dense notion in the definition of akrasia is the belief that there is an alternative course of action 'open' to the akrates. This condition is required in order to prevent the (immediate) assimilation of akrasia to cases of psychological compulsion-- cases where a person does not do otherwise because they cannot do otherwise. I shall not, however, attempt to explicate this notion. The difficulties that there are in setting out conditions for 'free', voluntary' action are everyone's problem; they are not special to accounting for akrasia.[1]

## 3. Practical judgment

The final condition to be briefly developed concerns the agent's judgment that, all things considered, another act would be better. This

---

[1] Michael Anthony Slote, "Free Will, Determinism, and the Theory of Important Criteria," Inquiry Vol. 12, No. 3 (Autumn 1969) pp. 317-338; Norton White, "Positive Freedom, Negative Freedom, and Possibility," Journal of Philosophy Vol. LXX, No. 11 (June 7, 1973) pp. 309-317.

condition has two parts: a) <u>what</u> it is that the akrates judges (the content of the judgment); and b) what it is <u>to judge</u> (rather than e.g., to think perhaps, to wonder, or to say) that another act is better. The nature of practical judgment itself will concern us in each of the succeeding chapters. Here I shall comment briefly on the content of the judgment.

To be a case of akrasia it must be the case that the agent judges that an act of a particular type is, all things considered, worse than an alternative. For some of the cases I have described, this is the obvious reading; for others it is less obvious. It is important to specify this for the unobvious cases lest we admit as akrasia cases which generate no intuitive puzzlement at all.

Let us assume, roughly, that the akrates judges the particular case in the light of some more general principle. Ella judges that she ought not to board this particular plane because, in general, life-endangering activities ought not to be undertaken for small gains (such as keeping an appointment, or not causing a scene). The smoker judges that she/he ought not to smoke this cigarette because smoking is dangerous, messy, expensive, and a nuisance to others.

Some general principles require one hundred per cent adherence, but many do not. Ella's general principle seems to, but the smoker's does not. Even one violation of Ella's principle can cost her life; but it takes several thousand cigarettes to endanger one's health, cost a significant amount, or make it likely that one will (need or want to) smoke in the presence of persons to whom it is annoying. One might easily judge "I ought not to be a smoker" (for all the good reasons that there are) and yet not judge "I ought not to smoke this cigarette here and now." The considerations which support the first judgment do not straight-away support the second. There is no inconsistency in judging the first and not the second. If one judges only the first, and not the second, one is not akratic in smoking this particular cigarette, here and now. Of course, "being a smoker" is not something other than smoking individual cigarettes with a certain (not very definite) frequency. But it is something other than, more than, smoking any particular cigarette.

The theoretical importance of this restriction is greater than the practical. "I ought not to be a smoker" does not entail "I ought not to smoke this particular cigarette." But there is good empirical evidence that any akratic smoker who wants to become a non-smoker would be well-advised to adopt the principle "I ought never to smoke any cigarette"--and this principle does entail "I ought not to smoke this cigarette here and now." This is because, given certain plausible psychological claims, the only way she/he will be able to act in accord with the first principle is to act in accord with the second. (For persons who are not smokers, but who smoke only occasionally, there is more leeway to adopt the strict, or the loose principle, as they wish.)

To summarize: Any ostensible case of open-eyed akrasia is in fact such a case if and only if it satisfies all these conditions: a) the act is strongly intentional, b) the real reason for the act is the akratic reason, recognized to be inadequate, c) the agent could have done otherwise, and d) the agent judges that it would be better not to perform an act of this very type. The skeptics deny that there are in fact any such cases; the believers assert that of course there are. The dispute cannot be resolved simply by producing such a case. This is due, in part, to the fact that we cannot 'prove', of any particular case, that it in fact satisfies all these conditions. My purpose rather is to investigate the theoretical issue: is it possible, or is it not, to produce an account of an act which (ex hypothesi) did meet all these conditions?

D. The Project From Here

As was indicated above (p. 13) a necessary condition on granting the existence of open-eyed akrasia is that we produce a coherent, preferably plausible account of it. One prime condition of adequacy on such an account is that it be compatible with a good general theory of action. Our task, then, is to consider whether open-eyed akrasia, as defined above, is compatible with a reasonable general theory of the explanation of action.

In order to clarify the prima facie conflict that akrasia presents, and to clarify alternative methods of resolution, I shall consider our general beliefs about action as codified in three philosophical theories of action--that of Goldman, that of Davidson, and one that is (arguably) to be found in Aristotle. Both Goldman and Davidson claim that open-eyed akrasia presents only an apparent conflict with their general theories. This conflict, it is claimed, can be resolved, without radically redescribing the _phainomena_. Within Aristotle's general theory, by contrast, the conflict seems to be irresolvable. Thus, the solution to our problem, of siding with the Socratic skeptics or with the believers in open-eyed akrasia will amount to determining which of these theories is the better general theory. A desirable additional feature of such a theory is that it suggest an account of the other side of our intuitions regarding akrasia; that is, that it suggest an account of our intuitive ambivalence.

This range of promising theoretical frameworks may usefully be schematized as follows. Consider Davidson's two principles, which seem incompatible with the existence of open-eyed akrasia:

P1  If an agent wants to do x more than he wants to do y and believes himself free to do either x or y, then he will intentionally do x if he does either x or y intentionally.

P2  If an agent judges that it would be better to do x than to do y, then he wants to do x more than he wants to do y.

Goldman accepts P1 and rejects P2. In company with Hume and Plato, Goldman sets out a 'want theory' of the explanation of action. Want theories are the most prevalent version, though not the only possible version, of a causal theory of action. A causal theory asserts something stronger than the claim that there _exists_ a causal account of all those events in the world which are cases of human action. (All the theories considered in this thesis are compatible with this claim, because they are all compatible with physicalism.) A causal theory asserts that the explanations of action we give, in terms of aims, purposes, reasons, wants, etc. are themselves causal explanations, having a structure similar in kind to explanations in the natural sciences. A want theory asserts that the crucial element in such a causal explanation is the invocation of a 'want' or 'passion' of one sort or another: we explain an action by citing a want, which is to be understood as a certain sort of antecedent psychological condition which causes the action.

Thus, P1 and P2 are interpreted by Goldman as setting out straightforward causal generalizations, connecting psychological states with one another and with action. The want theorist asserts that an act is caused by the strongest want, but denies that the strongest want is, in turn, caused by one's best judgment. One may or may not care enough about doing what's best on a particular occasion. Reason and passion may, and do, diverge. Thus, if this general theory is a good one, we would seem to have a straightforward account of open-eyed akrasia, provided only that it's true that the akrates most wants to perform the akratic act.

What we do not have, however, is an explanation of why a part of our intuitions seem to side with the skeptic. (We also, and more seriously, would seem hard-pressed to account for <u>enkrasia</u>--'strength of will'.) Davidson remedies this weakness of the want theorist. His account suggests an explanation both for open-eyed akrasia and for the Socratic side of our intuitions.

Davidson ostensibly accepts both P1 and P2. These principles together, we have seen, appear to show that it is false that there are open-eyed akratic acts. This is what our skeptical intuitions suggest. Davidson, however, argues that a Socratic account of akrasia is not in fact required by the truth of these principles <u>suitably interpreted</u>. It is a misunderstanding of the nature of the principles that accounts for our Socratic intuitions; a correct understanding of the principles enables us to account for open-eyed akrasia.

In contrast to the want theorist, Davidson does not interpret P1 and P2 as straightforward causal generalizations. Rather, he radically reinterprets them. Davidson's reinterpretation of the principles is so fundamental that I suggest we take him to reject both P1 and P2, and to substitute for them quite a different scheme for the explanation of action. (c.f. Chapter III) Davidson's claim, then, is that open-eyed akrasia is compatible with this new improved scheme of the explanation of action. Thus, if Davidson's new scheme is in fact a good one, and is preferable to some reasonable interpretation of P1 and/or P2, and if open-eyed akrasia is, in fact, compatible with it, we would seem to have an account both of akrasia proper, and an account of the Socratic side of our intuitions.

Some rather serious difficulties are located in both these general accounts and in their respective accounts of akrasia. We turn to articulate a better general theory; it bears close connections to Aristotle's account of action explanation. Several attempts to render open-eyed akrasia compatible with this good theory are considered and rejected. It is in the face of all these difficulties in rendering the believer's intuitions respectable that we are led to reconsider the account of the skeptic s,, and to investigate the theoretical background of the skeptic's account.

Aristotle's general theory, like Davidson's, ostensibly accepts both P1 and P2. Also like Davidson, and unlike the want theorist, he does not interpret these principles as straightforward causal generalization. Rather, for Aristotle, these principles articulate the formal structure of intentional explanation. This reinterpretation of the principles enables Aristotle to escape the most serious difficulties encountered by the want theorist. The modesty of the reinterpretation enables him to avoid Davidson's problems. It seems reasonable to conclude that Aristotle's account of action explanation is superior to the available alternatives, and has, in addition, independent virtues. This best theory seems to be incompatible with the existence of akrasia proper; thus Aristotle insists on some suitable <u>redescription</u> of the phenomenon.

Aristotle thus provides an account of the skeptical side of our intuitions, but at the cost of rejecting the more prominent and vociferous believer's side. Is such a result acceptable? Of course, when our intuitions are in conflict one of them has to give if the conflict is to be resolved. It also emerges, however, that the conflict between Aristotle's account and the believer's side of our intuitions is much less severe than has generally been thought; the skeptic's account need not be <u>all</u> <u>that</u> counter-intuitive. Still, a remaining implausible residue cannot be denied. Is this result acceptable? At this point, the problem about akrasia becomes one instance of the quite general problem of reconciling seemingly recalcitrant data with a good general theory. Aristotle's skeptical move here, of rejecting ostensible data disallowed by the theory, and redescribing it in a fashion which accords with the theory, parallels nicely common practice in related areas. Aristotle's strategy, in dealing with certain remaining implausible claims, would seems no less respectable than this common practice.

Aristotle's move mirrors the most common reaction of the practicing scientist when faced with experimental results which would tend to falsify a particular hypothesis being tested. The last thing the scientist does is to throw out the general hypothesis; well before that she/he musters all the ingenuity at her/his disposal to uncover an alternative explanation of the result and thereby an alternative description of the result. Thus, rather than 'disconfirming or falsifying instance' this unwanted pink precipitate is judged to be a case of contamination from a dirty test tube, or the expected result from the wrong solution, or the expected result from a solution of the wrong strength.[1] The reasonable practice of science is conservative with promising hypotheses; we strive to bring recalcitrant data into line with them.

An obstinate believer might, however, challenge this analogy. The scientist surely must have some reason to think the test tube actually was dirty, or the solution was of the wrong strength, if she/he saves the hypothesis with such an explanation of the precipitate. Without the possibility of independent checks on the nature of the data any hypothesis could be saved, and none would be reliable. We have already noted the absence of reliable checks on the various conditions specified in the definition of akrasia. (p. 25 above) Does not Aristotle thus override the recalcitrant data of resistant intuitions with all too much impunity?

Two further analogies can help to clarify and defend Aristotle's strategy. We are at times willing to override apparent data, for the sake

---

[1] Jane English develops this point in an unpublished paper.

of theory, even in the absence of independent checks. In both these cases the justification for rejecting the data is primarily the misfit with the favored theory *simpliciter* together with an alternate explanation of the data. One is the recent fate of the analytic/synthetic distinction; the other is a highly plausible (though still controversial) view of the physical sciences deriving from Thomas Kuhn.

Quine argued, in "Two Dogmas of Empiricism",[1] that, despite appearances, so-called 'analytic statements' are not in fact different in kind from ordinary empirical statements. Analytic statements, *qua* analytic, cannot be empirically defined; therefore there is no such thing. The statements we took to be analytic are in fact very general empirical beliefs, close to the center of the 'web of belief'. The Aristotelian skeptic might reason as follows: akrasia *qua* akrasia proper (more precisely, satisfying D above, p.14 ) cannot be reconciled with the best general theory of action; therefore there is no such thing. What we took to be open-eyed akrasia is in fact either unwitting unreasonableness, or the person could not help it (or it is unconsciously motivated . . .etc.) In both cases we reason from theoretic considerations to the denial of a seeming observation--or rather, to a redescription of the nature of what is observed.

Kuhn argued, in *The Structure of Scientific Revolutions*,[2] that there

---

[1] Willard Van Orman Quine, "Two Dogmas of Empiricism," in *From a Logical Point of View* (Cambridge: Harvard University Press, 1961), pp. 20-46.

[2] Thomas Kuhn, *The Structure of Scientific Revolutions*, (Chicago: The University of Chicago Press, 1962).

are no theory neutral observations even in physics. All observations are theory dependent, thus all are open to revision should they turn out to conflict with the best theory, or should our favored candidate for the best theory change. Events under descriptions are what a theory of the world is about; and the theory shapes (and limits) the descriptions of which those events may be instances. No event can be an instance of a description disallowed by the best theory. Similarly the Aristotelian might argue: anyone who believes there is such a thing as akrasia proper either believes an incorrect general theory (Goldman and Davidson), or has simply not noticed that open-eyed akrasia is disallowed by their general beliefs (The Underground Man). Given the truth of my general theory, it is clear that there can be no such thing. Let us turn now to consider these proffered accounts of akrasia.

CHAPTER II

MISTAKING THE WANTON FOR THE AKRATES

Perhaps the most natural first reaction in thinking about akrasia is to *explain* an akratic act simply by saying that the akrates momentarily lacked the desire to follow her/his better judgment; or, at least, that the desire to do the akratic act was 'stronger than', 'outweighed', or 'overcame' the desire to refrain. The akrates believes, to be sure, that refraining is best, but it does not follow that the desire to refrain is strongest. Quite the contrary.

> A trivial good may, from certain circumstances, produce a desire superior to what arises from the greatest and most valuable enjoyment: nor is there anything more extraordinary in this, than in mechanics to see one pound weight raise up a hundred by the advantage of the situation.[1]

Persons *act on* practical beliefs about what it is 'best' to do, it may seem, when and only when the *desire* so to act is strongest. Agreement between such practical beliefs and desires is by no means perfect. Persons act akratically, when they do, because of a certain kind of divergence between the actions recommended by 'reason' and by 'passion.'

This want theoretic account of akrasia is surely the most intuitively attractive account. It is also the most lucid. It therefore provides the most fruitful point at which to begin our investigation.

There is a large, and varied, tradition in philosophy, deriving from Plato and Hume, that would accept such an explanation as adequate,

---

[1] David Hume, *A Treatise of Human Nature* Vol. II, Introduction by A. D. Lindsay, (London: Dent & Sons Ltd., Everyman's Library, 1966), p.128.

and be justified in doing so, because the explanation of akrasia accords with its standard model for the explanation of all action. Davidson's P1, the 'motivational principle', is perhaps the least often criticized thesis in his piece. There are common, general beliefs about action that can seem so obvious as to be truisms that this sort of philosophical theory would justify: the strongest motive always prevails, the dominant desire determines action, we always do what we (most) want to do.

There are obvious attractions to such a simple strength of desire explanation of akrasia; and surely there is a sense in which it seems true of the akrates that she/he wanted to do the akratic act more, on this occasion, than to follow her/his better judgment. The point at issue, however, is whether this is an <u>adequate</u> <u>explanation</u> of akrasia. The answer to this is two-fold: a) is there a theoretically significant sense of 'most wants' such that it is plausible to claim, in particular cases, that the akrates does most want to perform the akratic act, and b) is the general theory a good one. The want theorist's account of akrasia will be explanatorily adequate only if the answer to both questions is affirmative. I shall focus on the most sophisticated and thoroughly elaborated version of a want theory that we have available--that set out by Alvin Goldman in <u>A</u> <u>Theory</u> <u>of</u> <u>Human</u> <u>Action</u>.

Before turning to Goldman, however, it will be well to set out briefly some of the intuitions behind the want theorist's account of action explanation. It is not, I think, accidental that want theories are the most prevalent version of a causal theory of action; nor that causal theories in general enjoy the popularity they do. Want theories exhibit numerous general features desirable in any theory of action. (Whatever the shortcomings of such a theory may turn out to be it is important to recognize the strong sources of its initial appeal.)

### A. Motivations to want theories

There are several sorts of considerations that can lead a philosopher of action to adopt some form of want theory. Some of these considerations provide better reasons than do others, and not all want theorists would admit to being moved by all of the considerations I shall suggest. However, I think it is worth setting out even those that would be disowned by some. I believe that the intuitive appeal of want theories, and thereby the intuitive appeal of their explanation of akrasia, derive from all of them.

The intuitive foundations of want theories fall into three rough areas: a) certain general theoretical ideals of explanation and understanding, b) a certain aptness in accounting for the experience, and reports of the experience, of 'inner struggle' by persons in acting, and c) certain logical features of our thought and talk about action in particular. I shall set these considerations out in turn.

a) There are generally believed to be systemmatic advantages to be gained by adopting some straightforward causal theory of action. If some causal theory can be made out, our knowledge of the world, human and non-human, will have a greater formal coherence than is allowed for by (most of) its competitors. There will be one general form of explanation in the natural and the human sciences, invoking a concept of causality which we "understand as well as any", or, in any case, "have to understand anyway". Unless explanations of the form "Susan did x for reason y" are understood causally it is urged that the nature of the explanation remains "totally mysterious". To attribute to such explanations a "sui generis" or "radically different" character from causal explanation can seem to do no more than to provide a new label for an 'explanation' that remains no less mysterious.[1]

There is a second systematic advantage, rarely emphasized by causal theorists themselves, to be gained by making out a causal theory. When persons act their bodies move. Actions and bodily movements do not map neatly onto one another. One may sign a contract with one's right hand, left hand, or feet; an arm rising may be a case of stretching, signaling, irritating one's neighbor, betraying the revolution. Still, there are at least vague limits to the bodily movements which could possibly be a case, say, of signing a contract. One could not be signing a contract if one's arm is propelling a tennis racket toward a tennis ball. Opponents of causal accounts have, quite rightly, insisted that there are factors outside the body of the agent which are also essential to the possibility of such an act (e.g. the institution of contracts), but their explanations have characteristically left it a brute but happy fact that

---

[1] Donald Davidson, "Actions, Reasons, and Causes," in Readings in the Theory of Action, ed. Norman Care and Charles Landesman (Bloomington: Indiana University Press, 1968), p. 187; Bernard Berofsky, "Purposive Action," American Philosophical Quarterly Vol.7, No.4 (Oct, 1970), pp.311-320; Stuart Hampshire, Thought and Action (London: Chatto and Windus, 1959), p. 166; William Dray, Laws and Explanations in History (Oxford: Oxford University Press, 1957); Charles Taylor, The Explanation of Behaviour (London: Routledge and Kegan Paul, 1965), p.5.

when one wants or intends to sign a contract one's body does <u>any</u> one of the range of things that could be a case of contract signing. Non-causal action explanations have characteristically <u>not</u> explained the occurrence of the bodily movement. Causal accounts, by contrast, at least purport to. If the factors in terms of which we explain actions (reasons, wants, beliefs) are the causes of the action, they are also the causes of the mere behaviour, since causation is extensional. The bodily movement is explained by citing its causation by <u>some</u> want (reason, belief); the action is explained by specifying <u>what</u> the want (reason, belief) was. Action explanations are just more detailed explanations of mere movement.[1]

Action explanations characteristically appeal to a range of psychological factors in the explanans. Jones' <u>reason</u> for hitting Smith was that Smith had insulted him. Madeline's <u>intention</u> in going to the convention was to look for a job. Tom is visiting his ailing aunt, rather than coming to the party, because he <u>believes</u> he ought. Mary has gone to New York because she <u>wants</u> to visit the galleries. The want theorist selects one of this range of psychological factors as privileged in explanation. Jones <u>acts on</u> that reason only because he wants to get back at Smith. Madeline's intention is to be explicated in terms of her <u>wanting</u> to get a job. Tom does what he believes he ought only because he <u>wants</u> to do his duty.

---

[1] Frederick Stoutland, "The Causal Theory of Action", in <u>Essays on Explanation and Understanding</u>, ed. Juha Manninen and Raimo Tuomela (Dordrecht, Holland, 1976), pp. 271-301.

The kind of systematic advantages to be gained from some causal theory of action can, I believe, be pressed to support the want theorists' move here. It can seem a natural extension of the original motivation to press the analogy with explanation in the physical sciences further. Crudely, causality in physics can be explicated in terms of a single predicate--that of energy. The notion of causal explanation is thus one of extreme generality. The notion of 'energy' provides a 'common coin' in terms of which we may explain events of diverse sorts--the flight of a rocket, the collapse of a bridge, nuclear and chemical reaction, as well as the outcome of a collision between billiard balls. Because such explanation invokes a single sort of explanatory notion, the relative effects of various causal influences on a particular event (state, process) are commensurable; the effect can be explained as some calculable function of the various causal influences. The 'parallelogram of forces' in physics is one clear case in point of such commensurability.

'Want', 'desire', or some kind of 'passion' can seem the most likely candidate in the psychological vocabulary to serve as such a 'common coin' in the explanation of action. Our pre-theoretic explanations of action frequently invoke comparisons which suggest a similar commensurability: "Why did you go to the convention after Christmas? I thought you wanted to go the islands." "I did, but I wanted a job even more."

Other psychological terms, such as 'reason', 'intention', 'practical belief' have seemed far less easily amenable to such comparisons. Jones may have reason both for hitting Smith, because he has been insulted, and against hitting him, because Smith is bigger and meaner than Jones. How are there considerations to be 'weighed'? Why is one acted on, the other not? Mary may intend to see the exhibition at the New York gallery, and also intend to go to the country with Sarah. But she cannot do both, because they happen on the same day. Why is one intention executed, the other not?

There have been attempts to force reasons for acting into commensurable form--from psychological hedonism to the postulation of 'ultimate practical principles'. For good reason, however, these attempts have not been widely accepted; as Davidson remarks "reasons for acting are irreducibly multiple."[1] But if this is the case, action explanation by reference to <u>reasons</u> as our primative causes would seem to be irreducibly disparate. The generality we legitimately seek in explanation seems better served by an appeal to wants at the basic level. We are then, of course, in a position to explain why some reasons are acted on, and others not.

The analogy with causal explanation in the physical sciences can be pressed even further by the want theorist. It can seem theoretically desirable not only that various psychological causes of action be commensurable, but also that they should be themselves 'energetic', 'forceful', and hence capable of <u>moving</u> to action. There is a natural aptness about describing 'wants' and 'passions', but not reasons, intentions, or practical beliefs in such dynamic terms. Feelings can 'press toward

---

[1] Davidson, "How is Weakness of Will Possible?," p.106.

expression', they can increase and decrease in 'intensity', they may be explosive'. There is a firm phenomenological basis for such attributions of 'energy' and 'force' to certain passions; and it seems intuitively obvious that psychological states such as intense desire and explosive anger affect our actions.[1]

---

[1] Exactly which metaphor for the motivating force of the passions is to be adopted has varied with the scientific climate of the theorist. Plato, in the Republic, and Aristotle, in the Nicomachean Ethics, sometimes personified the forces. Certain desires "urge the person aright. But there is another element which fights against and resists" these rational desires. (EN 1102b13). Some have felt, however, that an analysis of action which simply proliferates actors merely multiplies the problem to be analyzed. When Aristotle is speaking 'more precisely' he uses the analogy of 'spheres' moving with a certain force. When desires conflict, one "overcomes and pushes out" the other "like a sphere pushing another sphere off its course" (DA434a12-14). Schopenhauer favored a similar, but rather more abstract, notion. He likened desires to 'pure forces'. When a person has conflicting desires, that person is in the "situation of a body on which different forces act in opposite directions, until finally the decidedly strongest motive drives the others from the field" and determines the action. Freud suggested that desires have a certain 'affect charge', a notion which is to be used "in the same sense as the physicist employs the conception of a fluid electric current." The metaphor is yet more extended and sophisticated in Brandt's approving summary of current motivation theory:
> Various . . wants/aversions of the agent are <u>in force</u> at the time of action. These wants/aversions make contact with various ones of the conceived possible outcomes, which are states of affairs toward which the organism has wants/aversions; as a result there is generated a <u>psychological "valence"</u> of that state of affairs, positive or negative, <u>with a strength corresponding to the degree of strength of the respective want/aversion at the time</u> . . . Now we think of assigning numbers to the valence of an outcome and to the subjective probability of that outcome, given a certain action; and <u>the product of these numbers represents the 'expectable utility' of the action thought to lead to the outcome</u> . . . The size of the expectable utility may be represented <u>as a force-vector in the direction of the given action. The "law" of behaviour says, roughly, that the organism will take that action which conforms to the strongest force-vector</u> . . . The foregoing is only a simplified sketch of the relation between the intentional basic movements of a person and the values of certain variables characterizing him at the time. (Italics mine.)

Arthur Schopenhauer, Essays on Freedom of the Will, ed. and trans. by

Thus, for general theoretical reasons, the characteristics of commensurability and 'energy' would seem to favor an appeal to wants over other psychological features as the appropriate causal antecedents of action. These considerations would seem to support, and to be supported by, certain intuitions arising from our experience as agents, and as persons interacting with agents.

b) It seems intuitively plausible that one may have as many, and as 'vivid' thoughts as one likes about a course of action, or what it would be good to do, and not care enough to do it. It may, on occasion, be disconcerting, but seems a common enough human phenomenon, that, for example, Jones just doesn't care enough about his own physical well-being to suppress the urge to hit Smith. Tonight, Tom just doesn't care enough about his ailing aunt to postpone the party to visit her. These are things they generally do care about; generally such considerations move them to appropriate action. But, on occasion, the 'thoughts' do not have their usual 'feeling' accompaniment, and their 'inert and indolent' character, on their own, is painfully obvious.

Sometimes, in such a case, one feels conflicted, feels a struggle of, as it were, warring forces within. Sometimes one, sometimes the other,

---

Konstantin Kolenda, (New York: Liberal Arts Press, 1960), p.37; Sigmund Freud, "The Defense of Neuro-Psychoses" (1894) Collected Papers, Vol. 1, trans. J. Riviere, ed. E. Jones (New York: Basic Books, 1959), p.68; quoted in Judith Winter, "The Concept of Energy in Psychoanalytic Theory," Inquiry, Vol.14, Nos.1&2 (Summer 1971). p.146; Richard Brandt, "Traits of Character: A Conceptual Analysis," The American Philosophical Quarterly, Vol.7, No.1 (Jan 1970), p.28.

appears to be getting the upper hand. Practical beliefs seem a poor candidate for participation in such a struggle. At no time are they in any <u>doubt</u> as to what it is best to do; at no time do their practical beliefs begin to fail. (It has been centuries since any philosopher thought that any interesting cognitive or epistemological, much less motivational, point could be made in terms of 'strength and vivacity' of a <u>belief</u>.) Yet <u>something</u> with strength and vivacity seems to be occurring; and the strength of one of the members fails to be adequate to the strength of the other. Jones hits Smith, Tom neglects his aunt, when the desire to do the better succumbs to the strength of its opponent.

c) Finally, there is one central feature of our thought and talk about action which seems to support the want theorist's account of action explanation. Our action vocabulary draws an important distinction between the 'real' reason for an action, and other reasons which an agent may 'have', 'acknowledge' or whatever, but which are not in fact the reason for a particular action. The ordinary (not the philosophical) use of 'rationalization' depends on this distinction. It is claimed that some causal theory must be true if the significance of this distinction is to be intelligible.

For example, Tom may often visit his ailing friends out of kindness. On this occasion, however, the visit to his ailing aunt is motivated by a desire to stay in her good graces; this aunt is not only ailing, she is also wealthy and failing fast. The point is that in this case the visit is <u>due to</u> prudential financial interests rather than to kindness. This can be true even if Tom genuinely likes her, and even if he would have visited her anyway, out of kindness, had she not been rich. It is claimed that this distinction could not be made out, and no such account could ever be true, unless it is true that kindness in the one case, and financial interests in the other are the <u>causes</u> of the respective actions. The want theorist captures this distinction by saying that the desire to be kind, in the one case, and the desire to stay in the aunt's good graces, in the other, are the respective causes.

Thus, the want theorist can claim for her/his theory, and thereby for the straightforward explanation of akrasia that it provides, at least these advantages, desirable in any theory: a) systematic advantages of simplicity and generality both within action explanation, and in relating these explanations to explanations in the natural sciences; b) the ability to take seriously, and provide an account of certain reports of persons on their experience in acting--in particular, the role of desire and the place of conflict; and c) support from one central logical feature of our thought and talk about action.

Let us turn now to consider in detail the general theory of action proposed by Goldman, and the place of open-eyed akrasia within that theory.

### B. Goldman's <u>Theory</u> <u>of</u> <u>Human</u> <u>Action</u>:
### The Best Extant Account

The want theorist's account of open-eyed akrasia is simple and straightforward. Persons act akratically, when they do, because they most want to perform the akratic act at that time. Either they do not want to do the better at all, or they do not want to do it enough, for the time being. This account of open-eyed akrasia is clearly compatible with the general theory, which is neatly summarized in Davidson's P1: "If an agent wants to do x more than he wants to do y, and believes himself free to do either x or y, then he will do x, if he does either x or y intentionally."

Should this account be a good one, the possibility of open-eyed akrasia would be vindicated. In order to evaluate the explanatory adequacy of the account we need to consider two questions: 1) given the theoretically significant sense of 'want' within the theory, is the explanation plausible for a reasonable range of cases of akrasia?, and 2) is the general theory a good one? I consider these questions in relation to Goldman's version of a want theory because it is the most detailed and sophisticated such theory currently available.

## 1. Wants

We have, so far, spoken only vaguely of a want as a passion of one sort or another. The notion of a want is notoriously slippery.[1] In order to understand and evaluate the merits of any given want theory, it is essential to specify much more precisely the nature of this central theoretical notion. Goldman's characterization of these explanatory

---

[1] "The concept designated by the verb 'to want' is extraordinarily exclusive. A statement of the form 'A wants to S'--taken by itself, . . . conveys remarkably little information. Such a statement may be consistent, for example, with each of the following statements: (a) the prospect of doing X elicits no sensation or introspectible emotional response in A; (b) A is unaware that he wants to X; (c) A believes that he does not want to X; (d) A wants to refrain from X-ing; (e) A wants to Y and believes that it is impossible for him both to Y and to X; (f) A does not "really" want to X; (g) A would rather die than X; and so on." [Harry Frankfurt, "Freedom of the Will and the Concept of a Person," Journal of Philosophy, Vol. LXVIII, No. 1 (Jan. 14, 1971), p. 7.]

entities is the most thorough in the philosophical literature. According to him, wants are mental events, phenomenologically present to the agent, having a certain internal structure and comparative strengths. Persons are particularly good, though not infallible, authorities on the presence and nature of their own wants.

Goldman introduces a distinction between 'standing' and 'occurrent' wants; it is the latter only that cause actions. "An occurrent want is a mental event or mental process; it is a "going on" or "happening" in consciousness." A standing want is a disposition not merely to perform certain sorts of acts, but also to have corresponding occurrent wants. Thus, standing wants affect action by being 'activated' or 'manifested' in occurrent wants.[1]

Wants are theoretically distinguished from all the other 'goings on' in consciousness according to several criteria. Noting the similarity of his account to the widely attacked theory of volitions, or 'acts of will', Goldman first sets out two things that wants are not. They are not bodily sensations, for they have no phenomenal location. When I want to eat, the want is not (phenomenally) in my stomach in the way that a sensation of hunger is. The want is to be distinguished from the sensation; I can want to eat with no discernible sensation. Nor are wants a species of inner act. Goldman thus escapes the more powerful regress argument against the theory of volitions that has been pressed by Hume, Ryle, Melden, etc.

---

[1] Goldman, *A Theory of Human Action*, pp. 86, 88.

By way of positive characterization, Goldman addresses himself to 'want' used 'in a very wide sense'. "To have an occurrent want is to have an occurrent thought of x as attractive, nice . . . a favorable regarding, viewing or taking of the prospect of x."[1] The wants which are central to action explanation need not (though they may) be intense or emotion laden. Still, the relevant class is more delimited than the amorphous array indicated by Frankfurt. In particular, Goldman insists, no act is adequately explained until it is attributed to a want which is intrinsic--that is, a want for something found attractive in its own right.

One might say, for example, that John visited his ailing aunt because he wanted to. If he genuinely enjoys visiting her, then we have a want of the appropriate sort. If, on the other hand, the want to visit her is 'extrinsic'--wanted only as a means--to doing his duty or preserving his inheritance then, Goldman insists, we need something further. Otherwise we could not explain the fact that persons do what they regard as their duty, or otherwise worthy, on some occasions but not on others, occasions when "they are not much motivated" to do their duty, or whatever. One does one's duty, or whatever, when and only when one finds that prospect attractive. (Or, if one is too mean-spirited for that, when and only when one has a "negative feeling toward failing to do one's duty.')[2] Extrinsic wants are explanatory only when backed by a want (or aversion) which is intrinsic; it is only the latter which are themselves explanatory.

We have particularly good information regarding the nature of an

---

[1] Ibid., p. 94.  [2] Ibid., p. 53.

agent's wants through that person's own reports. As an item in conscious experience, wants are available to the persons who have them through "non-reflective self-awareness." That awareness contains "a kind of implicit knowledge" of the want. The agent need not 'look inward and see' what her/his want is: "When the desire is activated, I know what it is and [can] simply proceed to express it."[1] There is a "strong presumption" that the expression will be accurate.

Goldman is thus traditionally Cartesian in his view of first person knowledge of occurrent wants. This Cartesianism serves important theoretical purposes for the want theorist (c.f. p. 66 below). Still, it is prudently qualified in four ways. It is only *occurrent* mental events which are granted this special epistemological status; other persons are often as authoritative as I regarding my standing wants. Second, a person may 'not know what she/he wants' because she/he is *interested in* what her/his standing (stable, permanent) want on a given matter is, and it is not plausible to claim 'immediate knowledge' of these. Indeed, a person may not have any standing want regarding the matter at issue. Third, a person may not be able to *say correctly* what she/he wants because a a description she/he believes applies to the object of the want does not in fact apply, or the person does not know that description to apply. Or, the want itself may be vague and indeterminate, "a craving for I-know-not-what." Finally, "knowledge of one's occurrent wants is assured only during the moment of the want itself."[2] Hence, even if neither of the first two conditions obtain I may be unable to correctly express my want

---

[1] Ibid., pp. 96, 97.   [2] Ibid., p. 97.

a moment after it has occurred. I may have forgotten that I had it, or what it was.

Wants have comparative strengths. The effect, or lack thereof, of a particular want in causing action depends on a variety of other factors, particularly on the presence of other occurrent wants. "There are many occasions on which an action-want does not cause any action at all because some stronger want is present which 'overrides' the former one."[1] We have no <u>precise</u> measure for the strength of wants; still, <u>comparative</u> judgments can be made, by both first and third persons.[2]

<u>Qua</u> causes of acts, it is reasonable to suppose that wants cannot operate, as it were, 'at a distance'. They must 'shortly preceed' the acts they cause. Unfortunately, this general requirement on causes seems to generate a powerful number of phenomenological happenings, quite cluttering, it would seem, our conscious lives. Goldman's solution (a not entirely happy one) is to suggest that wants do not come in "discrete packages"; that is, there is no definite number that one has in a given time interval. "Not only is there no silent sentence corresponding to each . . . want, there is no other discrete 'impulse', 'throb', or 'flash' for each want."[3] Still, in accord with general features of causal explanation there are both 'upper and lower limits' to both length and complexity of an act that can be caused by a single want.

Because this feature is both theoretically important and potentially awkward--and because Goldman recognizes this--it is worth citing his view on this at length.

> There are projects that are too lengthy and complicated to be governed by a single occurrent want. They must be subdivided into smaller,

---

[1] Ibid., p. 113.  [2] Ibid., p. 50.  [3] Ibid., p. 95.

manageable parts, each of which must be preceeded by an occurrent want . . . [T]he project is executed by first forming an occurrent want for the entire activity, and then by forming occurrent wants for the various stages of the project at various appropriate times . . . In uttering a long and complicated sentence I may start with an overall desire to express a certain thought, without yet wanting to utter any specific words. A want to utter certain specific words to begin the sentence then forms, and additional wants for additional specific phrases are formed once earlier phrases are actually uttered.[1]

Thus, we have an admirably clear notion of the central explanatory entity that figures in Goldman's theory. Wants are datable events in consciousness, having a certain internal structure and comparative, if not (yet?) measurable strengths. They are not to be confused with bodily sensations or inner acts. And, we have unusually good, if not unshakable, evidence for the presence of particular wants in the testimony of persons having them. The elusive common notion of a want, evoked by Frankfurt, has been moulded into a sharp theoretical tool.

2. <u>Wants</u> <u>and</u> <u>explanations</u>

A want theory proposes an analysis of intentional action which is alleged to provide necessary and sufficient conditions, in psychological terms, for the occurrence of such action. The conditions are the following: a) there is some end the agent (most) wants; b) the agent believes that there is some behaviour in her/his repertoire which is either itself a realization of the end, or will result in the realization of the end; and c) the want, for the end, and the belief, about the behaviour that will realize it, cause the behaviour to occur. In Goldman's analysis, the end, which is the object of the want, is a want to perform an action of a particular sort.

---

[1] Ibid., p. 90.

There is a lacuna, however, between the assertion of a causal connection between events and the claim that the mention of one event <u>causally</u> <u>explains</u> the other. Causation is extensional; causal explanation is not. Amending slightly a remark of Davidson's:[1] the truth of a causal statement depends on <u>what</u> events are described; its status as a causal <u>explanation</u> depends on <u>how</u> the events are described. It is the <u>explanatory</u> <u>adequacy</u> of a want theory that is our main concern. How must wants, beliefs, and actions be described if the former two are not merely to cause, but causally <u>to</u> <u>explain</u> the latter?

For our purposes it is sufficient to note that subsumption under a covering law is widely agreed to be an important necessary condition of causal explanation, though it is, of course, far from sufficient.[2] Thus, if wants and beliefs are causally to explain the events they allegedly cause there must at least be covering laws under which descriptions of the actions and their antecedents are subsumable. Moreover, since explanation is not extensional, but depends on <u>how</u> the events are described, the laws themselves must be formulated in terms of wants, beliefs, and actions. This is required if explanations employing these terms are to be subsumable under them.

a) The philosophical context

Philosophers have made various attempts to provide covering laws,

---

[1] Davidson, "Actions," p. 191.

[2] Hempel, <u>Scientific</u> <u>Explanation</u> p. 273, note 33; Michael Scriven, "Explanations, Predictions, and Laws," <u>Minnesota</u> <u>Studies</u> <u>in</u> <u>the</u> <u>Philosophy</u> <u>of</u> <u>Science</u> Vol. III, ed. Herbert Feigl and Grover Maxwell, (Minneapolis: University of Minnesota Press, 1962). pp. 170-230; Israel Scheffler, <u>The</u> <u>Anatomy</u> <u>of</u> <u>Inquiry</u> (New York: The Library of Liberal Arts, Bobbs-Merrill Company, Inc., 1963) pp. 25-30.

in terms of wants, beliefs, and actions, under which (suitably filled out) action explanations would be subsumable. These suggested laws range from the extremely general to the utterly specific. The explanatory adequacy of most seems threatened by the familiar Scylla and Charybdis of falseness and vacuity.

Scheffler, for example, suggests laws of the form: "Whenever someone desires something, believing that it is contingent on something else, he performs that latter thing."[1] Now clearly, (as Scheffler notes) this law is not plausible as it stands: numerous cases spring to mind which would satisfy the antecedent but not the consequent. An agent may be <u>unable</u> to perform the desired act; an agent may want something else even more, which is believed by her/him to be contingent on performing some other, incompatible, action, etc. A reasonable impulse, in the face of such contingencies, is to build in a generous <u>ceterus paribus</u> clause. In this case, however, it seems that any <u>ceterus paribus</u> clause adequate to the task will be <u>so</u> generous as to render the 'law' vacuous. So many potentially falsifying contingencies are absorbed into its catholic scope that it becomes unclear whether <u>any</u> describable state of affairs would make us give it up. But if it is unfalsifiable, it is a poor candidate for an empirical law.

Hempel attempts to answer this worry about extremely general laws. We must, he argues, at least be able to formulate some more detailed laws (perhaps themselves subsumable under one like that above) if the

---

[1] Scheffler, <u>Inquiry</u> p.91

covering law model is to be shown to be adequate to action explanations. "Only the establishment of specific laws can fill the general thesis with scientific content, make it amenable to empirical tests, and confer upon it an explanatory function."[1] Hempel's suggestions do avoid ready falsification and also avoid an excessively generous ceterus paribus clause. The price of these virtues, however, is extreme specificity. And it seems probable that any law which built in enough specificity to avoid the obvious counter-examples would be satisfied by only one actual instance.[2] But if this is the case, an appeal to such a 'law' would seem to do no more than to reassert that the factors in terms of which the action is explained do causally explain it, via 'subsumption' under this highly specific law. The generality of the covering law would be a matter of form with little apparent content. But such an interpretation of the causal explanation of action would markedly distinguish it from explanation in natural sciences: there the generality of the laws is substantial. The claim to systematic advantages that prima facie favor the want theory would be undermined.

Davidson abandons the attempt to formulate causal laws of action in the face of problems such as these. To those who believe that our rough and generously qualified laws can be improved, at least in theory, Davidson replies:

> The suggestion is delusive . . . generalizations connecting reasons and actions are not--and cannot be sharpened into--the kind of law on

---

[1] Hempel, Scientific Explanation p.242. c.f. also pp.469-487.

[2] Ibid., p.481; VonWright, Explanation and Understanding p.25; Dray, Laws and Explanations.

the basis of which accurate predictions can be made . . . The laws
whose existence is required if reasons are causes of action do not,
we may be sure, deal in the concepts in which rationalizations must
deal . . . the classifications may even be neurological, chemical, or
physical.[1]

This move, however, is a radical one. It amounts either to the abandonment of a causal theory of action, or to a radical reinterpretation of the nature of causal explanation. That is, Davidson either would have to deny that wants and beliefs causally <u>explain</u> the actions they (may yet) cause; or he would have to claim that some explanations are respectable which are not backed by laws, formulated in the terms of the explanation itself. This is the view we consider in the next chapter. Goldman's reaction is more conservative. He attempts rather to patch up the laws with more localized remedies.

b) Goldman's account

Goldman insists that we should not expect <u>every</u> true description of an action to figure as a dependent variable of some universal law. It would be, he says, "foolish for psychologists . . . to try to formulate or discover laws for every act-property,[2] including checkmating one's opponent, turning on a light, or . . . pitching one's sixth straight shutout."[3] But he does not follow Davidson in denying that the covering laws will mention beliefs, wants and actions at all. Rather, he proposes

---

[1]Davidson, "Actions," pp. 193 and 195.

[2]This is but one of Goldman's technical terms that I shall simply quote, and in some cases adopt in exposition without comment. Much of this terminology marks substantive philosophical disagreement with my account and with those of other philosophers discussed, particularly on the individuation of actions. These differences however are not relevant to the matters that concern us.

[3]Goldman, <u>Human Action</u>, p. 76.

a rough covering law which mentions beliefs, desires, and <u>basic</u> acts in the explinandum.

> L. If any agent S wants to do A' (at t) more than any other act, and if S believes that basic act $A_1$ is more likely to generate A' than any other (incompatible) basic act, and if S is in standard conditions with respect to $A_1$ (at t), then S does $A_1$ (at t).

It is clear that L is not excessively specific: it thus escapes the risk, encountered by Hempel-like laws of probably having only one instantiation. On the other hand, L seems less likely to risk vacuity than Scheffler's very general candidate. The necessary <u>ceterus paribus</u> clause is less generous and less vague. The performance of basic acts leaves less to nature than does the performance of non-basic ones; 'standard conditions' require little more than that the agent be neither paralyzed nor bound hand and foot. L, moreover, is formulated so as to take account of other, conflicting, desires of the agent. L thus remedies two of the defects that have made philosophers skeptical about the empirical usefulness of most proposals for a general covering law of action.

There is a third line of criticism, however, that philosophers have mounted against proposed causal laws of action which could apply to L with as much force as to the previously rejected candidates. This is the claim that L is not a respectable causal law because it is 'analytic'. (Even Goldman remarks that L is "quite a good candidate" for being an analytic statement.) The criticism then runs that L is unfalsifiable not because of an exceedingly generous <u>ceterus paribus</u> clause, but rather because it makes no real claim about the world at all.[1]

---

[1]See for example: A. I. Melden, <u>Free Action</u> (London: Routledge & Kegan Pual Ltd., 1962); Raziel Abelson, "Doing, Causing, and Causing to Do," <u>The Journal of Philosophy</u> Vol. LXVI, No. 6 (March 27, 1969), pp. 178-192; Norman Malcolm, "The Conceivability of Mechanism," <u>The Philosophical Review</u> Vol. LXXVII (1968), pp. 63-72.

> . . . Suppose, then. that someone moves his finger and we propose as a causal explanation for this that he wanted to move it. How shall we, or the agent himself, decide whether this was in fact the cause?, . . . Our entire criterion for saying what he wanted . . . to do is what he in fact did; we do not infer the former from the latter on the basis of what we have in fact found.[1]

Nagel has argued that the extreme plausibility of (the likes of) L derives from linguistic practices only, and not from any extralinguistic facts. L appears to be true not because of the evidence we have for it, but rather because it reflects a deeply entrenched façon de parler.

> The claim that a desire underlies every act is true . . . only in the sense that whatever may be the motivation for someone's intentional pursuit of a goal, it becomes, in virtue of his pursuit, ipso facto appropriate to ascribe to him a desire for that goal.[2]

It is widely agreed that L is not falsifiable in the sense of yielding predictions which may then be tested for accuracy. It's analyticity, or 'merely linguistic' support would be one explanation of this fact. But this fact alone does not show that L is not a causal law. L is no worse off, in this respect, than many clear instances of causal laws.

> I know that on various occasions flying rocks cause windows to break, but I could not formulate any universal, predictively adequate law that related the occurrence of rocks flying with windows breaking. Similarly, many centuries before precise measurements for temperature were deveolped it was known that cold weather often causes water to freeze. But at that time no one was able to state a universal law that gives precise conditions under which water would freeze. People could have said that water freezes if it gets cold enough, but they

---

[1] Richard Taylor, "I Can," The Philosophical Review, LXIX (1960), cited in Goldman, Human Action p.111.

[2] Thomas Nagel, The Possibility of Altruism (Oxford: Clarendon Press, 1970), p.29.

could not have said how cold is cold enough.[1]

Falsifiability is a broader notion than predictive accuracy. When the former is unavailable, multiple connections within a theory will often suffice to vindicate the empirical usefulness of the law appealed to. The force of the flying rock may cause not only a broken window, but also a bruise on the nose for poor John inside; it was, moreover, forcefully thrown by Jane. The cold may cause not only the water to freeze, but also the tomato plants to wither; it was itself caused by a storm front descending from Canada. Such further connections are suggested by our theories about heavy flying objects and cold weather. When such related events occur, they provide evidence, independent of the breaking or the freezing, that it was forceful enough or cold enough.

With this notion of falsifiability at hand, it becomes clear that L escapes this last line of criticism as well. It's survival is due in large measure to Goldman's care in articulating the theoretically central notion of a want. The performance of a given act is never criterial of the ascription of a particular want.

> . . . there is normally a range of various possible (intrinsic) wants that might have caused a given act . . . it is always possible, at least theoretically, to account for [a piece of] behaviour by the postulation of some other (intrinsic) want.[2]

Nagel's claim is relevant not to the alleged 'analyticity' of L but to its truth or falsity. He is probably correct that 'desire underlies every act' is a deeply entrenched façon de parler. But it does not

---

[1] Goldman, Human Action, p. 73. Insofar as Davidson's pessimism about the possibility of 'laws of action' is based on their predictive uselessness, that pessimism is premature.

[2] Goldman, Human Action, p. 115-6.

follow from this that that is <u>all</u> it is. Some deeply entrenched ways of speaking are deeply entrenched precisely because they are widely believed to be <u>true</u>. The question for L is, given the theoretical connections Goldman provides for the notion of wanting (and thus the constraints on invoking particular wants in explanation), does L seem to be true?

We can now better appreciate the importance of Goldman's meticulous characterization of wants. Multiple connections within the theory are required in order to ensure the empirical content of L; and it is by following up these connections that we may evaluate its plausibility. Goldman sets out five reasonable sources of 'independent evidence' for the presence of the antecedent in action explanations.

First and most importantly there is first person testimony. If persons are highly reliable authorities on the contents of their own consciousness, and if occurrent wants are conscious happenings, first person avowals would provide particularly strong evidence, independently of the act, for the presence (or absence) of the events in a particular explanans. Taylor is right that there is no 'way' that the agent decides whether a particular want occurred; the agent does not depend on evidence (though the agent's brain may) in order to make this avowal. Nonetheless the agent can say, from an empirically priviledged position, whether such an event has occurred. Thus, first person avowals provide particularly good independent evidence for the truth or falsity of instances of L.

Co-temporal and sequential acts provide some evidence for identifying a particular want of an agent.

> If, for example, John was looking at the picture while he moved his hand, this supports the hypothesis that he wanted to adjust the pic-

ture. If, on the other hand, he was looking at the lamp [when he moved his hand and thereby flipped the switch] that tends to support the hypothesis that he wanted to turn on the light . . . . Sequences of acts are important in identifying an agent's purpose [want] because one often engages in an extended program of action all aimed at a single goal. (Each of the smaller action-plans will contain a desire to <u>help bring about x</u>, where x is the ultimately desired event.) An observer can attribute a prolonged sequence of action to a specific goal with more reliability than any single temporally proper part of that sequence.[1]

Other events, which are not acts, are also caused by wants, and provide further evidence for identifying a particular want. For example, if Sarah's facial expression is one of enthusiasm while repairing her car, that is some evidence for attributing an intrinsic desire to engage in that activity. If, on the other hand, her expression is one of annoyance, that is some evidence that she does not desire to engage in the activity itself, but desires only some result of it, probably acquiring cheaply a functioning car.[2]

We also know certain facts about the causes of wants. ". . . if I observe that S has not eaten for 16 hours, I have strong evidence that he will want to eat; and if I know that S hasn't slept for 40 hours, I can infer that he (probably) wants to sleep." Knowledge of an agent's likes, dislikes, and personality traits can provide evidence for her/his occurrent wants. "If I know that S likes chocolate ice cream, then I might guess that he will want to buy a chocolate ice cream cone at the ice cream parlor he has just entered."[3]

---

[1] Ibid., pp. 117-8.

[2] Goldman cites striking studies of the role of facial, vocal, and bodily cues which the observer cannot even indicate, that are nonetheless used by her/him in attributing particular emotions and desires to persons. Goldman, <u>Human Action</u>, p. 118.

[3] Goldman, <u>Human Action</u>, p. 119.

These, then, are some sources of evidence, independently of the action performed, for the ascription of particular wants to persons. They provide multiple connections within the theory, multiple ways to check on the truth of particular explanations. Goldman claims that they are sufficient to guarantee the empirical content and (rough) testability of instances of L.

> To be sure, we do not always have all the relevant information for making a want ascription with confidence. But there are some cases, probably many cases, in which our grounds for ascribing a particular want to an agent are as good as one gets in many empirical matters. In other words, we have 'adequate evidence'.[1]

Given his very full characterization of a want, Goldman is surely right that instances of L are not trivial in the sense of being either analytic or 'merely verbal' conventions.

### C. A Further Complication

The very feature of L, however, that made it less trivial, because more specific, than Scheffler's law may seem to auger yet a kind of triviality. The explanandum of L is a basic act--a turning of the hand, a moving of the foot, and not an insulting of Madeline, a cheating on an exam, a betrayal of a state secret. Sometimes, to be sure, we are interested in having basic acts explained, but our interest is more often, and usually more urgently, concerned with the explanation of non-basic acts. Goldman has said that it would be "foolish for psychologists to try to formulate or discover laws for every act property;" and he speculates that there may be "no laws dealing with many (perhaps all) of the properties of which higher-level act tokens are instances."[2] But if there

---

[1] Ibid., p. 119. [2] Ibid., p. 76.

are no laws dealing with non-basic acts, non-basic acts cannot be causally explained, in the traditional sense of 'explain' that Goldman is committed to. A theory that enables us to explain only hand-turnings and foot-movings, and not insultings, cheatings, and betrayals, would surely lack explanatory power we fairly expect in an adequate theory.[1]

An adequate theory need not provide laws dealing with every possible sort of non-basic act. Certainly, it need not produce laws which cover "checkmating one's opponent . . . or to take an even more extreme case, pitching one's sixth straight shut-out."[2] But the reason it need not is that these examples are very far from being 'nuclear cases' of intentional actions. We do not, characteristically, seek explanations in terms of reasons for them. This is because, unless one is Bobby Fisher or Sandy Koufax, they are not actions that one can perform reliably. It does not follow that an adequate theory need not provide laws covering kinds of non-basic acts for which we characteristically do seek explanation in terms of reasons; actions we can perform with some, if not perfect, reliability; the intentional actions we generally want to have explained. In particular, the akratic acts, the explanation of which is

---

[1] Goldman's theory of the individuation of acts is a complex and subtle matter that it would be beside our purposes to pursue. The difficulty arising from the fact that the explanandum of L is a basic act only, and not any higher-level act, independent of one's view of the relation between that basic act and the higher-level act--the same problem arises whether that relation is a certain kind of 'generation' between different events (Goldman) or whether it be identity under different descriptions (Davidson, Anscombe, etc.). The reason for this is that explanation is not extensional. Thus, even if the acts are identical (and just differently described), an explanation of the act under one description does not, characteristically, explain it under another. If they are not identical, the explanatory lacuna is even more obvious.

[2] Ibid., p. 76.

the central concern of this thesis, are practically always non-basic acts. If Goldman cannot explain non-basic acts in general, his theory will not enable us to explain akratic acts in particular.

Goldman acknowledges the need causally to explain at least some non-basic acts if his causal theory is to be shown to be adequate. However, he neglects, himself, to explain how they are to be explained within his theory. The reason for this may be that he is, at several points, not careful to distinguish 'cause' and 'causally explain'. Thus, while he succeeds in showing that non-basic acts are caused (if basic acts are), he provides no arguments to show that they can be causally explained. The lacuna left by Goldman can, however, be mended.[1]

Consider a non-basic act which wants explaining. Henry has insulted Madeline, and she demands an explanation. Because, he replies, she has tarnished his honor, and he wanted to avenge himself. L, slightly elaborated, provides the covering law under which an explanation of the utterance of the words can be subsumed. We may fill in initial conditions satisfying the antecedent of L as follows.

> Henry wants to avenge himself (at t) more than any other act [and he believes that insulting Madeline is more likely to generate his avenging himself than any other act] and he believes that uttering these words is more likely to generate his insulting Madeline than any other (incompatible) basic act (at t), and Henry is in standard conditions with respect to uttering these words.

From which may be deduced, and thus causally explained, "Henry utters these words." How are we to explain "Henry insults Madeline," the action that interests her? That action may be explained by appeal to a second, probabilistic, covering law, M, together with (our slightly elaborated) L.

---

[1] I am grateful to Robert Nozick for this solution.

M. pr(if one performs basic act $A_1$ (in certain circumstances) it will generate non-basic act $A^*$)=r, where r is _fairly_ close to 1.

The explanandum of M is the non-basic act that wants explaining; the explanans of M is provided by the explanandum of L. L and M together provide adequate covering laws for the causal explanation of the non-basic act of Henry's insulting Madeline. That act is intentional if Henry believes that uttering those words will generate insulting Madeline, and if that belief is part of a certain sort of causal chain that underlies L.

## 3, Want explanations and akrasia

As was indicated at the beginning of our discussion of Goldman, he does not offer an explicit account of akrasia. His remarks on irrational action in general, the genus of which akrasia is a species, cannot be invoked directly to provide an account of akrasia because they are themselves confined to cases of unwitting unreasonableness. I have selected his account of action in general because it nonetheless has the resources to provide a consistent and straightforward account of the 'nuclear case' of akrasia, viz. open-eyed akrasia. It is the clearest example in the literature of the kind of theory which, if adequate, would vindicate those of our intuitions which suggest that of course there is such a thing.

A certain affinity to the skeptics on the part of the want theorist should not surprise us. The difficulty with the skeptics view is not that cases of temporary 'ignorance' of overriding considerations _never_ occurrs. Clearly it does. And when it does, mention of the forgetting makes possible an easy explanation of the irrational act. The difficulty with the skeptics is their insistence that _all_ cases of irrationality _must_ exhibit this character (provided the act is intentional under that description and 'free'). The trouble is their insistence that there is not also such a thing as akrasia proper. Against this, experienced akrateis protest: there is such a thing as akrasia proper; sometimes they do the worse knowing full well that it is the worse.

This response fits well with a part of our pre-theoretic intuitions. We are inclined to credit such claims from others. It is central to Goldman's view that these claims are to be credited highly. After all, there is a strong presumption that these protesters <u>cannot be mistaken</u> about what they occurrently believe. And, there is often ample data for third person ascriptions of such occurrent beliefs. Beside first person avowals, there are often co-temporal and sequential acts: the closet drinker refuses to answer the door while indulging, or deliberately makes a spectacle of himself. There are facial and bodily expressions of unease, shame, or (sometimes) bravado. There is every reason to expect that Goldman would admit these phenomena as further evidence for an occurrent belief that the act is the worse, and thereby for the existence of open-eyed akrasia.

How then is open-eyed akrasia to be explained? Simply by pointing out that the akrates may know the act to be the worse but not care; the akrates may simply not be much motivated to do the better. Or, probably more often, the akrates cares about doing the better, but does not care enough. The want to do the better causes, e.g. the unease, the shame, or the bravado but "there are many occasions on which an action-want does not cause any <u>action</u> at all because some stronger want is present which 'overrides' the former one."[1] Actions are caused by the <u>strongest occurrent want</u>. Occurrent strength is a function of many factors beside the preference ranking either of the standing wants from which they are derived, or the evaluation of the respective objects.

Strength of desire is an important notion for the want theorist. The poor predictive powers of L (and M) are explained by Goldman by pointing to our paucity of accurate techniques for measuring the relative strengths of conflicting desires. This difficulty of measurement is exacerbated by the fact that "it cannot be assumed that the agent has a fixed intensity of desire for a given act throughout the course of the decision."[2] This very feature of desire--the fluctuation of strength to which it is prone--is not merely a nuisance to the want theorist however. While it could account for our difficulties with predictions, it also seems to make desire a particularly apt notion to invoke in the explanation of akrasia. Specifically, this very feature of desire enables us to explain certain sequences of acts which commonly surround one sort of akratic performance. Sometime akratic 'struggle' is not merely internal but is also acted out.

For example, an obese akrates Jack is beset by a desire for a chocolate eclair known to be waiting in the refrigerator. The desire to eat it causes him (<u>via</u> the appropriate chain of practical inference) to go into the kitchen. Along the way, a continent desire to not indulge materializes and overcomes the offending competitor. Resolutely, he leaves the kitchen, closing the door behind him. Still, the akratic desire nags, but the continent desire prevails. It causes him (<u>via</u>

---

[1]Goldman, <u>Human Action</u>, p. 113.   [2]Ibid, p. 107.

another chain of practical inference) to busy himself with activities, to distract himself, to fill his consciousness with other events, in hopes of blotting out or controlling the offending member. But the activities begin to bore him; he cannot keep his attention fixed. Free of competitors, the akratic desire comes, once again, to the fore. Without these allies, the continent desire is no longer a match for it. He returns to the kitchen and eats the eclair. Finally, the akratic desire became strong enough to cause the action.

Thus, Goldman has available an explanation of akrasia which fits the standard model for the explanation of all action. As with any other act, akrasia is explained by citing the strongest occurrent want, together with beliefs about how it will be satisfied. That explanation is an instance of L and M. The antecedent of the instance of L refers to the agent's wanting most, at t, to perform the akratic act; the explinandum of the instance of M refers to the akratic act. Moreover, the very features of desire which make it less than ideal for predictive purposes in general seem to make it especially suitable for the explanation of (one common variety of) akrasia.

I turn now to consider the plausibility of the general theory, and the place of the account of akrasia within it.

C. Scylla and Charybdis: Falseness or Vacuity

Goldman's version of a want theory takes important steps to avoid the familiar Scylla and Charybdis, falseness, or vacuity, which has plagued most other attempts to articulate such a theory. He does not, however, succeed. Despite its intuitive appeal, and careful articulation,

Goldman's accounts both of akrasia in particular and of action in general founders on just these shoals. The want theorist therefore does not successfully vindicate those of our intuitions which admit, even insist on, the existence of open-eyed akrasia.

1. The account of akrasia

The problem of vacuity arises for Goldman's account of akrasia in the following way. In the account of open-eyed akrasia, unlike the account of action in general, the notion of strength of desire, and comparative strengths of conflicting desire, must bear the whole burden of explanatory power. But that notion is not, within the theory, up to the task.

Goldman is sensitive to the fact that a want theory would be vacuous, in the sense of tending to be unfalsifiable, if there were not several sources of evidence, independent of the performance of the action, for the presence of the want which is causally to explain the action. His general theory escapes this danger because he is able to provide five sources of independent evidence for the ascription of the particular wants which are to figure in the explanans. However, the multiple connections which are supplied for wants simpliciter do not for the most part apply to the strengths of the wants. That is, most of these sources of evidence fail to provide any evidence for the ascription of that want with a given degree of strength, or even with a strength greater than the strength of some other (conflicting) want.

Consider the evidence that Goldman attributes to third persons, independently of the performance of the action, and of avowals of the agent. Co-temporal and sequential acts may provide evidence that there is conflict, as with our akrates Jack who walked into the kitchen, and then walked resolutely out again. But what is our evidence, independently of the dithering, for saying that first one, then the other desire was _stronger_? The co-temporal act, say, of contemplating the eclair is evidence only for the akrates' having some attitude toward it, since it holds his interest. That act is neither here nor there for determining which attitude, toward one and the same object, is stronger. A 'prolonged sequence of action to a single goal' merely suggests which desire _is_ being acted on. It does not provide evidence for the claim that it is acted on because it is the strongest; there is no evidence here that it _is_ the strongest. It is characteristic of conflicted action that facial and bodily cues convey conflicting messages. When one performs an action one _dislikes_ in its own right, but wants to perform for the sake of something else one wants, it is not uncommon for _these_ messages to convey only one's dislike of that activity. There is seldom any evidence for the strength of the want which is acted upon (which is 'stronger') from this quarter. If I know that Jack has not eaten for 16 hours, or not slept for 40, that is some evidence that he will want to eat and sleep quite a lot. But what is my evidence for the _greater strength_ of his desire to not eat, when he fails to do so under these circumstances, independently of the fact that he pops another diet pill (with a grimace), or stops for coffee in order to continue his cross-country drive?

Attribution of a desire with a given, relative, degree of strength has fewer connections with the general theory than does the attribution of the particular desire tout court. To that extent, it is a less satisfactory notion to bear the weight of explanation than is the notion of a want in general. Thus, explanations which depend essentially on an appeal to strength of desire--as the explanation of all cases of conflicted akrasia do--risk vacuity, even though the explanation of unconflicted action in general does not. Such explanations risk vacuity: they do not straightaway succumb. There remains one source of evidence, independently of the action performed, to which we might appeal. We have, Goldman says, an important source of evidence for the strength, as well as the mere presence, of the desire in first person avowals. The performance of the akratic act is thus not criterial of the akratic desire being stronger; an explanation of the act which invoked the strongest desire would not be 'analytic,' nor viciously circular.

But what evidence is actually to be expected from first person avowals? Would this evidence tend to confirm or to disconfirm the truth of the want theorist's account of akrasia? It seems that the want theorist escapes the Scylla of vacuity only to founder on the Charybdis of falsity in the account of akrasia.

Some akrateis, no doubt, would provide evidence which would tend to confirm the account. Jack, for example, might well say that he was simply overwhelmed in the end by the desire for the chocolate eclair. But there is, no less surely, an enormous range of cases in which the akrates would deny that there was any such strongest akratic desire. Some (few) of the airline passengers described by Lessing in the Golden Notebook[1] may have experienced a desire to avoid causing a scene, and thus a desire to board the airplane, in conflict with a desire to not board a plane they believed to be unsafe. The desire to board is, ex hypothesi stronger than the desire to not board: that is meant to explain the fact that they board the plane. But it seems very unlikely that these passengers would say that the desire to board was stronger than the desire to remain safely on the ground--stronger, that is, in any sense other than merely being the desire on which they in fact act.[2] Quite the contrary. One would expect them to report that their conscious lives were quite consumed with feelings of fear and desires to not board. And we as bystanders would have good reason to remark on the apparant phenomenological strength of the (allegedly) 'weaker' desire. It is causing other actions, such as glancing surreptitiously at other passengers, to see whether they will refuse--or else carefully avoiding their fearful glances.

Cases of strength of will, resisting temptation, present another range of cases where first person testamony would seem to undermine Goldman's appeal to strength. When one resists a chocolate eclair or a cigarette for the sake of health, or rises early from a sense of responsibility, one is seldom inclined to say that the desire to not eat or smoke, or the desire to arise, was a (phenomenologically) strong, lively, or

---

[1] c.f. p.20 above.

[2] 'Wants more strongly' is here used as interchangable with 'wants more', as Goldman would have it. I think this is both bad English and theoretically misleading. c.f. p. 81 below.

vivid one. When one is continent one characteristically resists bad and strong desire; one does what's best <u>despite</u> one's desire. Even if the want theorist's account were not falsified for (many cases of) akrasia itself, it would seem to turn a problem in accounting for akrasia into an equal and opposite problem in accounting for continence.

But perhaps the correct notion of strength is something rather more subtle than phenomenological color and noise. Goldman has emphasized that the wants to which he appeals are not to be confused with certain narrower uses in English. The wants which are causes of action

> . . . need not be intense or emotion laden, they need not absorb one's whole consciousness . . . Wants in general need be accompanied by no tension or bodily tone, such as that which characteristically does accompany wants which border on strong emotions.[1]

And Hume, also a want theorist, remarked on the obvious fact that persons "often counter-act a violent passion in prosecution of their interests", or indeed, counter-act a violent rational passion in acting akratically, as do the airline passengers. "It is evident, passions exert not the will in proportion to their violence, or the disorder they occasion in the temper." But this does not show that acts are not in fact caused by the strongest want. Rather, we must "distinguish betwixt a calm and a weak passion; betwixt a violent and a strong passion."[2] While it may well be reasonable to suppose that persons would sometimes disavow the greater <u>violence</u> of the passion on which they act, it does not follow that they disavow the greater <u>strength</u>.

But what is it for a desire to be both calm and strong; to be strong

---

[1] Goldman, <u>Human Action</u>, p. 49.  [2] Hume, <u>Treatise</u>, p. 130.

without being violent? What should we instruct the agent to attend to so as to test the truth of Goldman's account? There has been no substantial advance on this matter, to my knowledge, since Hume. He suggests that the strength of the desire acted upon is a matter of the agent's "general character and present disposition." For our purposes this gets us nowhere. An appeal to the "present disposition" merely re-labels the very feature that we need to have articulated. The "general character", by contrast, would seem to suggest that the passengers desire most strongly to not board the plane. They are not in the habit of risking their lives for social niceties. It is hard to see how to take advantage of Hume's distinction in testing the truth of Goldman's account.

This difficulty should not surprise us. Goldman's detailed characterization of wants as conscious (phenomenologically available) events is theoretically crucial for him. First person reports provide an important source of independent evidence for the presence of the antecedent in instances of L: it is just this evidence which preserves the the explanations from vacuity. First person reports are the only source of independent evidence for relative strengths of various wants; without them the explanation of any conflicted action would be vacuous. Now, I think that there is no natural understanding of the strength of a conscious happening dissociated from such phenomenologically obtrusive features. But more importantly, I think that such 'violent' features are what people mean to report on when asked about the strength of their desires. What confirming reports are available to Goldman seem to be made on this basis. It is some such thing, for example, to which Jack refers when he says that the desire to eat the eclair was stronger than the desire to refrain at the moment of succumbing. And first person reports are the only independent check that we have here.

The notion of strength of desire is crucial to the want theorist's account of akrasia. However the notion of strength here seems to serve them ill. If one interprets the notion straightforwardly, as a kind of phenomenological color, then it seems <u>false</u> that the akratic desire is always (or even often) the stronger. If, on the other hand, one recommends some other interpretation of strength, as Hume does, then one must explain the interpretation. This neither Hume nor anyone else has yet done. While unexceptionable as a <u>facon de parler</u>, the notion of strength of desire seems quite unable to bear theoretical weight. And even if someone were to provide an alternate interpretation of strength lacking these faults in the future it is unlikely that Goldman could exploit that account. It is not possible for him to reap the theoretical benefits of a Cartesian notion of a want in the general theory, and then throw away the awkward consequences to which that notion commits him.

The trouble with the account of akrasia runs broader than merely the notion of strength. Once the matter of the <u>plausibility</u> of the explanations is raised, very many proferred explanations seem quite implausible indeed, for other reasons. A comprehensive range of further problem cases is suggested by the group of akratic passengers at Orly.

---

[1]It seems much more plausible that persons always do what they <u>more</u> <u>want</u> to do than that they always do what they want <u>more</u> <u>strongly</u> to do. 'Wants more' is not in fact used interchangably with 'wants more strongly'. There seems to be no clear phenomenological interpretation of 'wants more' at all. A case of being misled by one's mechanistic (or hydraulic) metaphors for the mental?

(Nearly all cases of akrasia which fall outside the 'traditional class' set out in Chapter I suggest similar difficulties. c.f.p.17 above.) In very many cases it seems likely that persons would disavow <u>any</u> <u>want</u> <u>at</u> <u>all</u> to board the believed unsafe airplane, and not merely disavow a <u>strong</u> <u>want</u> for that end.

There is only one passenger in the whole group for whom Goldman's account does seem plausible. It is certainly possible that the cool doctor experienced a desire to keep his appointment in London, believed that boarding was the only feasible means to that end, and therefore wanted to board the plane. On the plausible assumption that he believed not risking his life to be the better course he is akratic. But it is highly implausible to imagine most of the other passengers experiencing any such <u>desire</u> to board the plane.

For some of them it certainly seems that their conscious lives are consumed with feelings of fear; for others, entirely occupied with speculation (of the sort Anna engages in) that they are perhaps suicidal, and thus not akratic after all. It seems highly probable that many passengers would insist that there just <u>was</u> <u>no</u> <u>(conscious)</u> <u>event</u> <u>at</u> <u>all</u>, with respect to boarding, and <u>ipso</u> <u>facto</u> no desire to board. If there had been, according to Goldman, they ought to have known, quite effortlessly.

For other passengers, perhaps most, there may well have been phenomenological happenings regarding boarding. But what kind of happenings? <u>Not</u> an <u>attraction</u> to boarding, most likely, locked in struggle with an attraction to refusing, an act tending to preserve their lives. Nor even an attraction to obeying orders or to not causing a scene, and thereby an 'extrinsic' desire to board. Some probably felt simply that failing to heed the loudspeaker's order is something one just does not do. There is a (believed irrational) feeling of the inevitability of leaving such decisions to specialists; a (believed irrational) intimidation by the 'authority' of the complicated system of air travel.

Is one too afraid to disobey? Would one be just too embarrassed by the scene caused by refusal? Does one fail to protest for some other reason? It is probable that many persons could not answer. Both the nature and the object of the attitude might well be unclear. Coming to identify such complex responses is a sophisticated achievement in self-knowledge. The notion of comparative strength is rather unclear in the relatively straight-forward case of desire; its difficulties would be multiplied several fold in application to such obscure and complicated responses, which also seem to motivate action. I think that many persons would often be at a loss what to avow regarding either the nature, or the strength, of their attitudes toward boarding or refusing to board. Therefore the testamony of such persons would seem to falsify the explanation of the want theorist; they might well insist that they did not want to board at all, much less very strongly.

In sum, then, the want theorist's account of akrasia seems inadequate because it is highly implausible for a wide range of cases of akrasia. It seems not to be true that every case of akrasia is (immediately) preceeded by any such mental event as a want to perform that act. When such events do occurr, it is often not the case that comparative judgement of strength can be made, or even quite make sense. And even when such events do occur, and comparative judgments of strength are possible, the strongest want is not well corrllated with the act which is actually performed. Persons sometimes counteract a 'violent' passion even in acting akratically.

2. The general theory

These latter objections to the account of akrasia, of course, suggest straightforward generalization to the theory of action taken as a whole. Goldman's version of a covering law theory of action escapes vacuity largely due to the meticulous characterization of wants, and to all the sources of independent evidence provided to determine their presence. But it is precisely because of this fact that the theory seems easy to falsify. Instances abound where the required causal antecedents just don't seem to be there. In some cases it seems that the conscious event 'shortly preceeding' the action is not a want, but rather some other attitude. In others, there seems not to be any (pertinent) conscious event at all.

These objections, if sustained, would be quite lethal to the theory. They would undercut explanations not merely in the subset of cases where the act was not preceeded by a want. Even for cases where it is true that one did what one wanted most strongly to do, the strongest want would not be the explanation of the act. The generality fairly sought in a reasonable theory would be lacking. For those cases where the conscious happenings are present the phenomenology would be, as it were, epiphenomenal to the explanation. Goldman attempts to defuse these objections. His failure is instructive.

In many cases actions are explained not by citing <u>a want</u> for any object, but rather by citing some other attitude. One of the theoretical advantages enjoyed by want theories was suggested (p.47) to be the 'common coin' it provided for the explanation of actions of various sorts. That is, the want theorist attempts to analyze these other attitudes into wants. The data to be accounted for by a theory of action, however, seem, at first blush, to contain distinctions which are resistant to such reduction to a common coin. Goldman considers the objection that his theory obliterates the distinction between doing something because you want to do it, on the one hand, and doing something intentionally (even though you hate doing it) out of a sense of duty on the other. The point of course can be generalized to other motivations, such as those of the passengers at Orly.

He insists that the distinction is not <u>obliterated</u> because a want to do one's duty, or to board the plane for whatever reason, can be distinguished from wants of other sorts. The multiplicity of apparent motivations is superficial; they are all <u>wants</u>, though wants of different sorts. The genus 'wanting' must be involved in all actions, though the species may vary.

> The 'attractiveness' of doing one's duty is not that of going swimming on a hot day or of seducing Claudia Cardinale. (But then, the attractiveness of going swimming on a hot day is not the same as the attractiveness of seducing Claudia Cardinale either.)[1]

But some airline passengers, we have suggested, would surely insist that

---

[1]Goldman, <u>Human Action</u>, p. 53.

the prospect of boarding the plane was not attractive to them at all. They boarded for an entirely different reason. Goldman is willing to allow this provided they will admit to a "negative feeling toward failing" to board. He argues that this does not damage his theory for the following reason:

> Whenever an agent acts in order to avoid or prevent an aversive occurrence of x, there is a sense (or use) of the term "want" in which we can say that he wants to avoid x or prevent x.[1]

Goldman's defense is quite insufficient: the objection to the wan theorist's reduction stands. It is just not plausible that persons apparently motivated by something other than a want would always grant any such negative feeling toward failing to do what they do. Even in cases where they would, we do not have a 'common coin' for a negative feeling is not a want. Most importantly, the sense in which we can say that this negative feeling (when present at all) is a 'want to avoid' is not Goldman's sense of want at all; rather it is the highly promiscuous sense outlined by Frankfurt; Goldman is not entitled to invoke it on pain of vacuity. In sum, no good reason has been provided to believe that apparently diverse motivations are all species of the single (theoretically significant) genus, wanting. The burden is on the want theorist to show this. Indeed, it remains unclear what the force of the claim amounts to.[2]

The second objection is more sweeping. It seems not to be the

---

[1] Ibid., pp. 53, 51.

[2] Nelson Goodman, "Seven Strictures on Similarity," Experience and Theory, ed. Lawrence Foster and J. W. Swanson, (Amherst: University of Massachusetts Press, 1970), pp. 19-30.

case that every act is (shortly) preceeded by a conscious event of any relevant sort--whether a want or some other attitude. Indeed, our phenomenological lives would be really quite extraordinary if Goldman's theory were true. Consider briefly the phenomenological consequences of Goldman's (well-motivated) urge to 'fill up the causal space' between high level desire and action.

> In uttering a long and complicated sentence I may start with an overall desire to express a certain thought, without yet wanting to utter any specific words. A want to utter certain specific words to begin the sentence then forms, and additional wants for additional specific phrases are formed once earlier phrases are actually uttered.[1]

It is surely quite mad to posit 'felt attractions' for even long phrases intervening between a want to say something (when even _this_ is conscious) and the saying of it. One just _does_ utter first one phrase, then another, normally with _no_ further (pertinent) phenomenology at all. It seems patently false that the information processing involved in such an action passes through one's consciousness at all; the information just _gets_ _processed_. First person reports in general would surely come much closer to Anscombe's description than to Goldman's:

> . . . it is not in all cases that 'I did so and so in order to . . .' can be backed up by 'I _felt_ a desire that . . .' Suppose I feel an upsurge of spite against someone and destroy a message he has received so that he shall miss an appointment. If I describe this by saying 'I wanted to make him miss that appointment' this does not necessarily mean that I had the thought "If I do this, he will . . ." and that affected me with a desire of bringing it about which led to my doing so. This may have happened but it need not. It could be that all that happened was this: I read the message, had the thought "That unspeakable man!" with feelings of hatred, tore the message up, and laughed.[2]

---

[1] Goldman, _Human Action_, p. 94.

[2] Anscombe, _Intention_, p. 17.

Goldman credits highly first person reports of their experience; he makes theoretical hay out of their accuracy. Yet he seems strangely insensitive to the fact that what most persons are likely to report, in a wide range of cases, it the absence of any want in consciousness. This important problem simply will not be solved by such weak defenses as a claim that "it all happens very fast" of course, or a reminder that the accuracy of first person avowals is defended only during the moment of wanting itself.

> . . . upon remembering an act that you performed, but failing to remember an occurrent want that might have caused it, you should not conclude straightaway that there was no occurrent want that caused it. You may well have forgotten having had that occurrent want.[1]

Such a thing, of course, is possible; but Goldman must establish a far stronger claim. The burden is on him to show that there are such phenomenological happenings--not merely that there might be. This burden he has not discharged; and we have no other reason to believe in them. Indeed, I suggest that it is not a promising line to pursue further.

A very popular move at this point is to weaken the notion of a want. Most want theorists, indeed, do not suggest that the causal antecedents of action are phenomenologically given. They do not insist that they be available to the agent through introspection, they do not grant the agent sufficient authority on their presence or absence to enable her/him to falsify particular explanations. Wants are to be treated like theoretical entities.

There is something right in this move. It surely seems that not

---

[1] Goldman, Human Action, p. 98.

all plausible psychological attributions are present in (or mirrored) in phenomenology. And the grounds for ascribing these states seem more complex than merely looking inward. But the more permissive want theorist tends to simply introduce whatever want is wanted to account for particular acts. No reasonable alternative account of adequate evidence for the presence and nature of the want has yet been proposed. In view of this, more permissive interpretations of the covering laws escape falsification only at the price of quite obvious vacuity. Goldman took an heroic course in attempting to avoid this difficulty. But the price he paid was desperate implausibility.

\* \* \*

Despite its initial attraction, we must reject the want theorist's account of action explanation, and with it the straightforward account of open-eyed akrasia. The explanation of akrasia, claiming that the akrates wanted more to perform the akratic act seems false for a wide range of cases. And this move, if it had been successful here, would simply have transformed a difficulty in accounting for akrasia into an equal and opposite problem in accounting for 'strength of will'. Should the notion of 'want' be weakened to avoid this criticism, the explanation looks vacuous.

The criticism of the account of akrasia is connected to a mirror-image criticism of the general theory. The theory proposes covering laws which connect action with psychological antecedents. But either the antecedents seem simply not to be there, or falsity is avoided by weakening the laws to the point of vacuity. The actual grounds of psychological ascription, it seems, have not been attended to. At least this much is clear: those grounds are more complex than mere introspection; and those grounds, whatever they are, suggest that open-eyed akrasia is _more_ problematic than the want theorist would have it. In particular, our intuitions about psychological ascription balk at so impotent a notion of evaluation and practical judgment. Wants and practical judgments seem not to be attributable in splendid isolation from one another. Our intuitions find open-eyed akrasia at least somewhat puzzling. There is, after all, the Socratic side. This the want theorist has ignored. Davidson attempts to account for it. Let us turn now to consider this second, more sophisticated, attempt to provide an account of open-eyed akrasia.

CHAPTER III

THE DAVIDSONIAN AKRATES

Davidson's article "How is Weakness of Will Possible?," is largely responsible for the recent resurgence of philosophical interest in akrasia. His account of open-eyed akrasia is dense, difficult, and strikingly lacks intuitive appeal. Nonetheless, both the account and the general strategy are important.

This account is the first explicitly to place an account of akrasia within the context of a general theory of action. The philosophically most difficult class of akratic acts is carefully articulated. Davidson self-consciously avoids the want theorist's dilemma of falseness or vacuity in setting out the general theory. He interprets P1 and P2 as something other than straightforward causal generalizations. Suitably interpreted, he argues, these principles are compatible with the existence of open-eyed akrasia. But it is easy to misinterpret them. It is when misunderstood that the principles appear to rule out the possibility of that phenomenon.

In this chapter we consider Davidson's account in detail. It is *prima facie* preferable to the want theorist's account in this respect as well. The want theorist simply discounts the Socratic side of our intuitions regarding akrasia. Davidson, by contrast, focuses, explains, and then attempts to explain them away. Davidson provides not only an account of open-eyed akrasia, but also an account of why we half-doubt that it exists.

First we set out the Davidsonian context, the explanation for the fact that there is a <u>prima facie</u> difficulty about akrasia. Then we set out Davidson's solutin to the difficulty. This solution has two parts: an explanation of akrasia and action at the macro level (using the psychological vocabulary) which is novel, subtle, and complex, combined (uneasily) with explanation at the micro level (the level of neurophysiology). This second part of the solution leans heavily on certain doctrines of token materialism and the anomoly of the mental. Finally, we evaluate the merits of the account, both of akrasia and of action in general.

## A. The Intuitive Problem

Davidson proposes a (by now famous) paradigm case of akrasia, designed to focus on the theoretically most difficult kind of case. This is an akratic plight to which both the <u>sturm und drang</u> of strong feeling and the stern eye of duty and morality are simply irrelevant.

> I have just relaxed in bed after a hard day when it occurs to me that I have not brushed my teeth. Concern for my health bids me rise and brush; sensual indulgence suggests I forget my teeth for once. I weigh the alternatives in the light of the reasons: on the one hand, my teeth are strong, at my age decay is slow. It won't matter much if I don't brush them. On the other hand, if I get up, it will spoil my calm and may result in a bad night's sleep. Everything considered I would do better to stay in bed. Yet my feeling that I ought to brush my teeth is too strong for me; wearily I leave my bed and brush my teeth. My act is clearly intentional, although against my better judgement, and so is incontinent.[1]

There is a problem about the possibility of such an action

---

[1] Davidson, "Weakness of Will" p.101-102.

because the belief that such an act could occur appears to be incompatible (as we have seen) with P1 and P2. P1 asserts the connection between wanting and acting that the want theorist rightly emphasized, but wrongly over-emphasized.

> P1: If an agent wants to do x more than he wants to do y and believes himself free to do either x or y, then he will intentionally do x if he does either x or y intentionally.

P1 is not sufficient to capture the form of action explanation. Thus Davidson supplements it with P2, the principle which was simply denied by the want theorist.

> P2: If an agent judges that it would be better to do x than to do y, then he wants to do x more than he wants to do y.

Davidson says that P2 expresses a 'mild' form of internalism; but it is in fact a rather strong one. It is not as strong as Socratic internalism, which seems to assert that judgements of value are the sole determinant of desire, but it certainly says more than that judgements of value "must be reflected in wants (or desires or motives)."[1]

Davidson hints at some possible lines of defense of P2, against the want theorist's denial, and a certain counter-intuitiveness but he also expresses many reservations about the truth of either P1 or P2 just as they stand. He asserts, but does not argue, that the apparent conflict between the two principles and the admission of open-eyed akrasia "will survive new wording, refinement, and the elimination of ambiguity."[2]

Davidson can afford to be a bit cavalier in the expression of the principles. This is because his strategy is to show that akratic

---

[1] Ibid., p.98.  [2] Ibid., p.96.

acts, in the sense defined, can be admitted even if we accept P1 and P2 in their current form. His intent is to undermine the <u>motivation</u> of philosophers of diverse persuasions to attempt to deny either one of the principles, as our want theorist did, or the possibility of open-eyed akrasia, as Socrates and Aristotle did. Contrary to appearances, Davidson claims, P1, P2, and the admission of akratic acts are not in fact incompatible. That they do appear to be incompatible, of course, explains those of our intuitions that are Socratic.

This strategy is to be preferred to further attempts to refine or defend the principles for two reasons: a) "Tinkering with them does not yield a satisfactory account of incontinence" in any case.[1] The want theorist's tinkering with P2 has, I hope, been sufficiently undermined. And b) "a common and important mistake about the nature of practical reasoning"[2] underlies our tendency to think, falsely, that these three theses are incompatible. It is this mistake which explains our Socratic intuitions.

Davidson's account of this mistake, and his suggested remedy, comprise the heart of his own 'solution' to the problem of akrasia. It involves no less than a radically reconstructed account of the nature of practical reasoning in general. Thus, Davidson suggests, the strategy of reconciliation will both exhibit an important truth about the nature of practical reasoning, and will provide an account of the real nature

---

[1]Ibid., p. 102.   [2]Ibid., p. 96.

of open-eyed akrasia. A flat-footed denial of P2 or D does neither adequately.

The trouble, as well as the intuitive plausibility of P1 and P2, derive from "a very persuasive view of the nature of intentional action and practical reason," according to Davidson. Though persuasive, it is emphatically not the view he accepts in this article.

> When a person acts with an intention, the following seems to be a true, if rough and incomplete, description of what goes on: he sets a positive value on some state of affairs . . .; he believes . . . that an action, of a kind open to him to perform, will promote or produce or realize the valued state of affairs; and so he acts (that is, he acts because of his value or desire and his belief).[1]

Let us call this theory-sketch 'A'.[2] The view is certainly prominent in modern theory of action. Anscombe defines an intentional action as one done for a reason. And Davidson himself, in several other contexts, seems to subscribe to a similar view. In "Actions, Reasons, and Causes" he accepts this definition of an intentional action, and suggests that the reason explains the action by rationalizing it.

> A reason rationalizes an action only if it leads us to see something the agent saw, or thought he saw, in his action--some feature, consequence, or aspect of the action the agent wanted, desired, prized, held dear, thought beneficial, obligatory, agreeable.[3]

---

[1] Ibid., p. 102.

[2] Davidson suggests (wrongly, I think) that the view derives from Aristotle; but it certainly is a picture suggested by fixation on the practical syllogism. The major premise of the syllogism specifies the valued state of affairs; the minor premise the belief that circumstances are ripe for realization of that state of affairs; and the conclusion is an action, when the premises are combined "straightaway (the agent) acts." [But let us reserve a discussion of Aristotle's theory of action for its own context (Chapter V).]

[3] Davidson,"Actions,"p.179.

Now, given this desire and this belief, the agent is in a position to infer that the performance of the action is desirable. But additionally, "given this desire and this belief, the conditions are also satisfied that lead to (and hence explain) an intentional action . . . . There is no distinguishing the conditions under which an agent is in a position to infer that an action he is free to perform is desirable from the conditions under which he acts."[1]

But, says Davidson, such a view of practical reason and intentional action "contradicts the assumption that there are incontinent actions."[2] The agent judges that staying in bed has much to be said for it, yet it is not the case that straightaway he stays in bed. Rather, he rises and brushes, an action incompatible with staying in bed.

Is such an action in fact ruled out by A? I should think not. Davidson does, after all, set a positive value on the state of affairs of having healthy teeth, and believes that brushing them contributes to that end. Thus, according to A, the conditions are satisfied which lead to, and explain, the rising and brushing, and thereby the akratic act. The explanation fits the general model of intentional action perfectly.

P1 and P2 may derive some of their plausibility from A, but quite

---

[1] In "Freedom to Act" Davidson made the identity of these conditions criterial of an agent's being <u>able</u> to perform acts of a given type. "A can do x intentionally (under description d) means that if A has desires and beliefs that rationalize x (under d), then A does x." [Donald Davidson, "Freedom to Act," in <u>Essays on Freedom of Action</u>, ed. Ted Honderich (London: Routledge and Kegan Paul, 1973]. p. 148.

[2] Davidson, "Weakness of Will," p. 103.

clearly, they impose stronger requirements on an adequate explanation than does A. P1 and P2 <u>add</u> to the characterization in A the requirement that the agent acts to realize the state of affairs which is <u>more</u> valued, and not merely valued. A ignores, and cannot account for, the effect on intentional action of an agent's having more than one value. It is thus inadequate as a sketch of intentional action. P1 and P2, by contrast, suggest one way in which a system of values may be related to action.[1]

Secondly, A is inadequate as a sketch of practical reason. Practical reason is involved not merely in acting on a reason, but also in coming to a conclusion about what to do. Our theory must enable us to express the fact that we are able to take into account more than one consideration that is recognized to bear on a particular context of action. Practical reason can recognize not only that there is <u>something</u> to be said for doing x, but also that there is, not infrequently, also something to be said for doing some other action, the performance of which is incompatible with performance of x.

These are two quite separate flaws in A. First, A apparently provides sufficient conditions for the <u>performance</u> of any action for which the agent believes there is something to be said. This is clearly bizarre. Second, it represents the (intellectual) function of practical reason as simply noting disparate reasons for and against a given course

---

[1] Davidson's view seems to have changed from "Actions, Reasons, and Causes" where he explicitly disavowed such systematic connections: a reason, he says there, "must not be taken for a conviction, however temporary, that (the action) ought to be performed, is worth performing, or is, all things considered, desirable." ("Actions," p. 180.)

of action, with no indication that these reasons can be weighed, compared, and a reasoned conclusion be reached. Davidson confounds these two issues in suggesting that "this picture of moral reasoning is not merely inadequate to account for incontinence, it cannot give a correct account of simple cases of moral conflict."

> The situation is common; life is crowded with examples; I ought to do it because it will save a life, I ought not because it will be a lie; if I do it I will break my word to Lavinia, if I don't I will break my word to Lolita and so on. Anyone may find himself in this fix, whether he be upright or temporizing, weak-willed or strong.[1]

It is not the case that A cannot account for conflicted or incontinent action. Such actions can be explained in A; they are not explained correctly because they are explained too easily. A provides sufficient conditions not only for the rising and brushing, and breaking his word to Lolita; it _also_ provides sufficient conditions for staying in bed, and breaking his word to Lavinia. Indeed, even cases of conflict represent this difficulty with A as being too special, too localized. A cannot explain the <u>non-performance</u> of any act for which there is recognized to be something, however little, to be said. It would seem hardly ever to be the case that there is only _one_ value recognized to be realizable in a particular context: I ought to stay at the table because I enjoy relaxing after dinner; I ought to arise and depart because "La Strada," which I adore, is playing at the corner. I ought to remain in the living room because I enjoy the decor here; I ought to retire to my bedroom because I enjoy the decor there. There need be _no_ consideration

---

[1] Davidson, "Weakness of Will," p. 105.

intrinsically _against_ any of these possible actions in order to generate the logical problem, except for the fact that I cannot do both it and another, also desired, action. Since it is impossible to perform all the actions for which, according to one's values, there is something, anything, to be said, the theory seems to provide sufficient conditions for a logically impossible state of affairs. Thus, the first problem with A arises for cases of incontinence, conflict, and a host of others.

The second difficulty with A, however, is the one highlighted by considering cases of conflict. Clearly a theory of practical reason must enable one to express the fact that persons can weigh various considerations, and arrive at practical conclusions on the basis of such weighing. The need for such a function is particularly acute in a case of conflict, for typically, the conflicted person recognizes considerations for and against the performance of an action, but does not (yet) know how they add up; the person has not reached a practical conclusion. Akrasia, by contrast, does not put pressure on the theory at this point. The akrates, _ex hypothesi_, has come to a conclusion, on the basis of all the considerations.

Davidson, however, appears to think that the flaws are connected. It is in virtue of misunderstanding the relation between disparate reasons and practical conclusions that A yields contradictory predictions and vacuous explanations of action. Hence, correcting the account of what it is to come to a practical conclusion (a problem which is not obviously relevant to the explanation of akrasia) can help to correct the account of what it is to act intentionally. Since akrasia is a case of intentional action, this is precisely what we need in order to provide an explanation of akrasia.

There is some reason to think that the flaws are connected. The explanation of an action will sometimes need to, and always may, refer to such a weighing (the steps by which the deliberative conclusion was reached) as well as to the deliberative conclusion itself. "I thought telling the lie was best, all things considered" is not always a satisfying explanation of a lie. One wants to know what the considerations were, and how they added up that way. This is the point at which the want theorist introduces the notion of strength of desire. The various considerations correspond to desires of varying strengths, and one performs the action which is most strongly desired.

Davidson, by contrast, insists that the weight, and potential efficacy, of various reasons cannot be reduced to commensurable form in this way. "Reasons for acting are irreducibly multiple."[1] Our resistance to the want theorist's introduction of a single measure, strength of desire, might be construed as a non-moral analogue of Davidson's rejection of a 'single moral principle.'

Davidson favors a distinction between "prima facie desirable (good, obligatory, etc.)" and "absolutely desirable (good, obligatory, etc.)." An action that has something to be said for it, that there is a reason to perform, is prima facie, but not 'absolutely' desirable. The reason is a consideration to be weighed by practical intellect, but it does not follow that it is a reason that will be acted upon. Once

---

[1] Ibid., p. 106.

this distinction is recognized, the account does not represent practical reason as issuing contrary directives, logically impossible of fulfillment. "x is better, prima facie, than y (because I enjoy x)" does not conflict with "y is better, prima facie, than x (because I have promised to do y)." A prima facie practical judgment is not a directive to action at all. In order to come to a practical conclusion, and to have any reasoned directive to action, "It is not enough to know the considerations on each side; [one] must know how they add up."[1]

Now how, according to Davidson, do they get added up? How does practical reason move from its function of noting reasons for and against doing x, and reasons for and against doing not-x, to a conclusion about what to do? And how does practical reason become "practical in its issue and not merely in its subject matter?" Davidson's account from this point on is dense, difficult, and subtle. His strategy of reconciliation, aimed at showing that a correct understanding of the nature of practical reason will 'solve' the problem about akrasia, turns on an extended analogy with probabilistic reasoning. Probably it can be interpreted in diverse ways;[2] I shall simply opt for what seems to me to be the most obvious. I shall consider one strand of argument that is there, and consider its adequacy to the task that Davidson has set himself.

---

[1] Ibid., p. 106.

[2] See for example Gilbert Harman, "Davidson on How Weakness of Will is Possible," unpublished paper, and Paul Grice, "Probability, Desirability, and Mood Operators," unpublished paper.

B. The Solution: The Weatherman Approach

What is central to the solution of the problem of incontinence proposed in this paper is the contrast between conditional (prima facie) evaluative judgments and evaluative judgments sans phrase.[1] Since it was a misunderstanding about the nature of practical reasoning that led to our difficulties about akrasia,[2] presumably the distinction is also crucial to a correct understanding of practical reasoning in general. What is this distinction? What does it say about practical reason? And how does it solve the problem of akrasia?

1. The picture of practical reason

Individual reasons for an action, disparate reasons for and against performing it, presumably yield conditional (prima facie) evaluative judgments, and not evaluative judgments 'sans phrase.' Action, however, is "geared directly to unconditional judgments."[3]

The alleged difficulty with (the mistaken) theory A was twofold. First, on that view, there was no way for practical reason to combine and add up these individual and disparate considerations. It could merely note that there was this to be said for the action, that to be said against it; but "we can hardly expect to learn whether an action ought to be performed from the fact that it is both prima facie right and prima facie wrong."[4] Second, that view left unexplained the fact that not all recognized considerations were, or indeed could be, acted upon.[5]

"The real source of the difficulty" with this view of practical

---

[1] Ibid., p. 111.   [2] Ibid., p. 96.   [3] Ibid., p. 110.
[4] Ibid., p. 108.   [5] Ibid., p. 104.

reasoning, Davidson now suggests, is that the prima facie conclusions, (e.g. "This act is prima facie right" and "This act is prima facie wrong") have been "detached from the principles that lend them color"[1]--presumably exactly what is to be said for, what to be said against, performing the action. Clearly, one must have available the grounds of the various prima facie judgments if one is to come to a reasoned conclusion as to how they add up. And, one might expect there to be some connection between this capacity of practical reason to add up various considerations, and the explanation of the fact that some considerations are acted upon, while others are not. ". . . [the agent's] reason for doing a rather than b will be identical with the reason why he judges a better than b."[2]

Practical reason, in its function of coming to conclusions, is misconstrued if formalized in terms of 'practical syllogisms', subject to operations using the logical rule of modus ponens. Rather the form of such reasoning is to be depicted using a 'prima facie' operator, which operates on "pairs of sentences related as [expressing] moral judgment and ground."[3] A practical judgment sans phrase, by contrast, is one which is not governed by the prima facie operator. There is thus a difference in 'logical form' between practical judgments based on particular reasons and practical judgments involved in action for a reason.

Formal characteristics of 'prima facie' practical judgments can be illuminated, Davidson suggests, by considering an analogy with

---

[1] Ibid., p. 108.  [2] Ibid., p. 110.  [3] Ibid., p. 109.

reasoning from probabilistic evidence.  In such a case, we are not entitled to reason from two true premises:

    M1   If the barometer falls, it almost certainly will rain.
    m1   The barometer is falling.

Via <u>modus ponens</u>, to the conclusion:

    C1   It almost certainly will rain.

At best, we are entitled to conclude "That the barometer is falling renders it probable that it will rain."  '$P \rightarrow Q$' is not the correct logical form of M1; detachment from M1 is prohibited; no conclusion can be categorically asserted (even when suitably qualified by 'almost certainly').

    The argument for this is straightforward.  Consider an instance of probabilistic reasoning to a contrary conclusion, which could, in some circumstances, be no less valid:

    M2   Red skies at night, it almost certainly will not rain.
    m2   The sky is red tonight.
    C2   It almost certainly will not rain.

Valid arguments from true premises guarantee the truth of the conclusion.  Assuming circumstances in which both sets of premises are true, both C1 and C2 would be true.  But there seems to be good reason to think that they cannot be, that they are contraries.  The following seems a plausible, if rather rough, principle to accept regarding such statements:

    I.   Almost certainly not-p  $\rightarrow$  not(almost certainly p)

C2, by I, would entail not(C1); C1 and C2, by I, would entail a contradiction.  Thus, they are contraries; both cannot be true together.

    It should be noticed that C1 and C2 are not contradictories.  C2 is not equivalent to the negation of C1.  The following is not a plausible principle:

II. not(almost certainly p) $\longrightarrow$ almost certainly not-p

Indeed II is quite certainly false. We may know nothing whatsoever in regard to either p or not-p. When this is the case we should be warranted in asserting the antecedent but surely not the consequent. Both C1 and C2 may be false; it may be utterly uncertain what will happen; but between pairs of contradictories both cannot be true, and both cannot be false.

The weaker relation of contraries, however, is all that is required in order to generate the logical trouble for the above formalizations of probabilistic reasoning. In a context of falling barometers and nocturnal red skies, each (separate) piece of evidence may support a probabilistic prediction to a different state of affairs; the predictions themselves would be contraries. Therefore the reasoning must be invalid as represented. The form of probabilistic reasoning cannot be captured correctly in syllogistic form, and the conclusions do not have the form of C1 and C2.

"The way to mend matters," Davidson suggests, "is to view the 'almost certainly' of(M1 and M2) as modifying, not the conclusion, but the connective."[1] Thus, probabilistic predictions are to be schematized in the following way:

M3 pr(if the barometer falls it will rain)
m3 The barometer is falling
C3 pr(it will rain,M3 and m3)

---

[1]Ibidl, p. 108.

    M4   pr(red skies at night, it won't rain)
    m4   The skies are red tonight
    C4   pr(It won't rain, M4,m4)

This formalism enables us to express, without logical difficulties, the probabilistic predictions of contrary states of affairs that seem to be valid under the circumstances. C3 and C4 are each supported by a part of the evidence, and they are logically compatible.

Davidson argues that '*prima facie* practical conclusions' are to be interpreted in a similar fashion. "In logical grammar '*prima facie*' is not an operator on single sentences, much less on predicates of action, but on pairs of sentences related as [expressing] moral judgment and ground."[1] Thus, a sample of practical reasoning is misconstrued if understood in the following way:

    M5   If an act is one of lying, it is better not to perform it than
         to perform it
    m5   A is an act of lying
    C5   It is better not to perform A than to perform it

The reason that this would be incorrect is parallel to the case of probabilistic reasoning. Consider a piece of practical reasoning to a contrary conclusion:

    M6   If an act is one of mercy, it is better to perform it than not
         to perform it
    m6   A is an act of mercy
    C6   It is better to perform A than to not perform it

But C5 is the contrary of C6; both cannot be true together. (Both, of course, may be false. It may be quite indifferent whether one performs an action or refrains from performing it.) Surely 'A is better than B' entails 'It is not the case that B is better than A.' Thus, C5, by

---

[1]Ibid., p. 109.

this principle, entails not(C6). The judgment that one has reasons both for and against performing a given action, if construed in this way, cannot be expressed without contradiction. Rather, practical reasoning, at this level, is to be understood as follows:

 M7 pf(x is better than y, x is an act of lying and y is refraining from an act of lying)
 m7 A is an act of lying and B is refraining from lying
 C7 pf(B is better than A, M7,m7)

 M8 pf(x is better than y, x is an act of mercy and y is refraining from an act of mercy)
 m8 A is an act of mercy and B is refraining from an act of mercy
 C8 pf(A is better than B, M8,m8)

Again, this formalism enables us to express, without logical difficulties, the fact that we may legitimately recognize considerations both for and against performing a given action. Both conclusions can be true together, and this is what was required. Practical conclusions are not categorical judgments, or statements; rather they are '*prima facie*' judgments or statements; their correct expression includes the grounds on which they are asserted.

 Neither probabilistic judgments nor practical judgments are confined to considering only one piece of evidence, or one isolated consideration, at a time. Indeed, Davidson emphasizes that for purposes both of predicting the weather and deciding what to do, none of the above samples of reasoning will be of nearly as much interest as the probabilistic, or *prima facie*, judgment which is based on <u>all</u> the believed relevant considerations. A prediction, or a decision, based on all the relevant information will be a better prediction, or decision, than that based on only some; but consideration of all the relevant evidence does not change a conditional probability prediction into an unconditional, categorical one, nor a <u>prima facie</u> practical judgment into an 'unconditional' one. In the case of weather prediction, the judgment we aim for is C9: pr(rain,e) or pr(not-rain,e), where 'e' is all the available evidence. In the case of a practical judgment, the judgment we aim for is C10: pf(a is better than b, e), where 'e' represents all the believed relevant considerations.

One of the flaws Davidson charged the rival theory with was that it failed to provide the means to explain how practical reason could determine not merely what the relevant considerations were, but how they added up. Does Davidson's model do any better in this regard?

Davidson, surprisingly, seems happy to grant that his account is <u>no</u> better off, in this respect, than the rejected theory. He moves swiftly through three claims of increasing strength from the trivial and obvious claim that neither the probabilistic, nor the practical, judgment based on all the relevant considerations C9 or C10 'follows logically' from judgments based on individual considerations--through the more interesting, and controversial, claim that "in neither case do we know a <u>general formula</u> for computing how far and whether a conjunction of evidence statements supports a conclusion from how far and whether each conjunct supports it." He concludes with the quite extraordinary admission that "we have no clue how to arrive at [the likes of C10] from the reasons."[1] To be sure "its faulty prototype (in the rival theory] was in no better shape," but it was in no worse shape either. Davidson's

---

[1] Ibid., p. 109.

formalism remains better off in that it enables us to <u>express</u> conflicting considerations without contradiction, but we are no better able to <u>resolve</u> the conflict.

Are we to understand Davidson's account of akrasia to exploit this (alleged) lack of 'logical' or indeed any kind of connection between a consideration of the various reasons and the way that they are added up? Are we to represent the akrates as exercising the prerogative, now formally granted him, of forming the all-things-considered judgment to do A rather than not-A, despite his recognition that not-A is supported by better reasons? Is the behaviour to be 'explained' by reminding us that <u>neither</u> A nor not-A follows from the premises; hence there is nothing more <u>outré</u> about his concluding A than about his continent cousin concluding not-A, all things considered? The reasons for not-A may be better than the reasons for A, but he is not, 'logically', or in any other way, thereby required to conclude not-A.

Fortunately, this is not Davidson's solution. The definition of akrasia, after all, attributed to the akrates the judgment that, <u>all things considered</u>, it would be better to do not-A than A. The slip twixt the lip and the cup is not to be located here. We do not know <u>how</u> the akrates arrived at the judgment, all things considered; we do not know from Davidson's account how practical reason ever serves that function, or even if it does. But we do know <u>that</u> the akrates did so conclude.

In fact, no practical judgment <u>based on considerations</u> amounts to the 'unconditional judgment,' the 'practical judgment <u>sans phrase</u>,' that Davidson says is crucial to the account of akrasia, and to an understanding of practical reason. To repeat, and emphasize, a previous point: consideration of all the relevant evidence does not turn a probabilistic prediction into an unconditional one, nor a prima facie practical judgment into an 'unconditional' one, according to Davidson.

Davidson's conditional/unconditional distinction seems primarily intended to remedy the first defect of theory sketch A, rather than the second; and the flaws seem not to be connected after all.[1] That theory was inadequate not only to express and explain the fact that practical reason comes (somehow or other) to practical conclusion, it also failed to account for why some considerations caused actions and others not-- how any consideration entertained could fail to be executed. "There is no distinguishing the conditions under which an agent judges that an act she is free to perform is desirable from the conditions under which she acts."[2] Even if Davidson's theory can offer no greater illumination about how decisions are reached, he appears to think that the conditional/ unconditional distinction captures the difference between concluding that an action is to be done and executing that conclusion. According to Davidson, it is precisely the characteristic of prima facie judgments that enables them to express conflict without contradiction (a virtue) that precludes those judgments from being relevant to the execution of all things considered judgment. " . . . the conditionalization that keeps [C7] from clashing with [C8] and [C10] from clashing with either, also insulates all three from action." "Reasoning that stops at conditional

---

[1]Davidson,"Weakness of Will," pp. 8-9.   [2]Ibid., p. 102.

judgments such as [C10] is practical only in its subject, not in its issue."[1]

What, then, is the reasoning which is "practical in its issue?" What is an unconditional practical judgment? Oddly enough, it seems to be a judgment which precisely *is* 'detached from the premises that lend it color.' Rather than the connection we expected, it is a sharp distinction that Davidson exploits. "Intentional action, [he has] argued in defending P1 and P2, is geared directly to unconditional judgments like 'It would be better to do a than to do b'."[2] Davidson's other name for unconditional judgments, used interchangably with that term, is 'practical judgment *sans phrase*.' The name seems to reinforce such 'detachment' from any reasons which could support it. It is a practical judgment which says no more than what ought to be done; it does not say why, does not mention its grounds. It is not governed by the 'pf' operator. For some reason, unspecified by Davidson, it is such judgments that are involved in action: "Practical reasoning," he insists "does arrive at unconditional judgments, otherwise there would be no such thing as acting on a reason."[3] It is an unconditional judgment which provides the reason on which the agent acts.

2. <u>Solution to the problem of Akrasia</u>

It is clear that this machinery enables us to resolve the

---

[1] Numbering of the conclusions is adjusted for the numbers of the examples in this text. Ibid., p. 110.

[2] Ibid., p. 110.  [3] Ibid., p. 110.

contradiction between P1,P2, and the admission of akratic acts in the sense defined. Davidson claims that it also provides the correct solution to the problem of akrasia.

> . . . now there is no logical difficulty in the fact of incontinence, for the akrates is characterized as holding, all things considered, that it would be better to do b than to do a, even though he does a rather than b with a reason. The logical difficulty has vanished because a judgment that a is better than b is a relational, or prima facie, judgment, and so cannot conflict logically with any unconditional judgment.[1]

This 'solution' is subtle enough to warrant more care in spelling out. P2 mentions an unconditional, not a prima facie, judgment: "If an agent judges that it would be better to do x than to do y [simpliciter] then he wants to do x more than he wants to do y." By P1, it is this unconditional judgment on which the person acts. The definition of akrasia, by contrast, mentions only a prima facie judgment, "the agent judges that, all things considered, it would be better to do y than to do x." A conditional, or prima facie, judgment cannot logically conflict with an unconditional one. Thus, the akrates may be described, without contradiction, as making the following two compatible judgments: "It is better to stay in bed than to rise and brush, all things considered" [pr(a is better than b, e)], but "it is better to rise and brush than to stay in bed simpliciter" (b is better than a). Furthermore, doing b is intentional; it is done for the reason provided by the unconditional judgment. Originally, this slight difference in the judgments attributed by the various principles went unnoticed. Attention to the analogy with probabilistic reasoning has shown that this small verbal difference

---

[1]Ibid., p. 110.

bears enormous theoretical weight; indeed, all the theoretical weight. One might well wonder whether it is up to the task.

C. Criticism of the Solution

I think that there are at least four separate respects in which Davidson fails to make good his claim to have 'solved' the logical problem about akrasia. I shall discuss them in turn. 1) The account is highly implausible. No good reason is provided to tempt us to accept it despite its implausibility. 2) Even for the tiny fraction of cases to which it might, implausibly, apply, the account is not sound. Davidson misuses the analogy with probabilistic reasoning. The analogy fails at several, crucial places. 3) Finally, whatever phenomenon it is that Davidson may have accounted for, akrasia is not a part of it. Any phenomenon reasonably fitting Davidson's description would not be intentional; but akrasia, by definition, is intentional.

1) There are many attitudes toward the akratic act that it is surely plausible to attribute to the akrates: she/he may be attracted to staying in bed, or to eating the hot-fudge sundae; she/he may want to do it; the airline passengers may be afraid, embarrassed, or otherwise disinclined to refuse to board. The one attitude it seems most implausible to attribute, however, is the one that Davidson requires: it is just not plausible to suppose that the akrates judges at all, much less categorically (!), that the akratic act is better. The very closest we may plausibly come is to attribute the judgment that the akratic act is better some (but only some) things considered. For

obvious reasons, this is not an attribution that Davidson could either welcome or exploit.

There is "no paradox" Davidson claims, in "supposing that someone holds that all he believes and values supports a certain course of action, when, at the same time, those very beliefs and values cause him to reject that course of action", causing her/him presumably to judge 'unconditionally' that the akratic act is better. For reasons to be developed below, I suggest that we read out Davidson's remarks about this peculiar 'unconditional judgment' that the akratic act is better. We would do better to interpret him as claiming that there is no paradox in supposing that the judgment that 'y is better than x, all things considered' __causes__ the agent to __do x__, and omit reference to another, intervening __judgment__, which turns out to be so problamatic.

2) Davidson represents the akrates as judging that "all things considered, it would be better to do y than to do x" and also as judging that "it would be better to do x than to do y" __simpliciter__. Perhaps, just perhaps, there are some such cases of akrasia. But even if the contradiction has been eliminated for cases of which this is true, the contradiction reappears in two, no less plausible, and clearly more prevalent, sorts of case.[1]

The contradiction reappears for an akrates who judges, no less plausibly, that "it would be better to do y than to do x", rather than "it would be better to do y than to do x, all things considered." And,

---

[1] This point is also made by Harman in the paper cited above.

it reappears for cases fitting Davidson's definitiom precisely if we substitute for P2 the equally plausible principle P2':

> P2': If an agent judges that, all things considered, it would be better to do x than to do y, then he wants to do x more than he wants to do y.

Of course, these two ways of re-encountering the contradiction do not seem to be very different. This suggests both that the problem may be generalized, and that Davidson's 'solution' is in fact as suspicious as it looks at first glance. Consider Harman's new principle, P4:

> P4: If an agent judges that, all things considered, it would be better to do x than to do y, then he judges that it would be better to do x than to do y.[1]

Harman is surely right that P4 is even more plausible than either P1, P2, or the assertion that there are akratic acts fitting Davidson's definition. P4 is about as close to a 'logical truth' as any statement is. The explanation for this is straightforward. All statements about what an agent judges are--either implicitly or explicitly--relative to reasons, that is, relative to some or to all things considered. The analogy with probabilistic reasoning should have made this clear. If one says "Probably it will rain," as one may say "It would be better to stay in bed," the relevant considerations are unexpressed, but they are surely to be understood. What is, or ought to be, meant is that all things considered, it will probably rain; there simply is no reasonable judgment "Probably it will rain" simpliciter. A judgment of 'better'

---

[1] Harman, "Davidson," p. 5.

sometimes also leaves the considerations unexpressed; but there is no more reason to think that judgments of 'better' are not always relative to certain considerations than there is to think that probabilistic judgments are not always relative to certain considerations. Davidson is simply wrong if he thinks that judgments of 'better' are not always relative either to some or to all the considerations.

There is clearly much that is illuminating in the analogy with probabilistic reasoning. There is also, it seems, much potential for confusion through misinterpretation. It is offered, after all, as an analogy, and not as a model which is isomorphic throughout. Since the analogy appears to bear so much weight in Davidson's argument, it merits closer attention. There is reason to think that Davidson has misused, as well as used, the analogy. The analogy <u>fails</u> to hold in several crucial respects that Davidson needs to explit. Thus, even for the small fraction of pre-theoretic cases of akrasia to which the account might (implausibly) apply, that account is not sound.

3) Let us return to the 'solution' as Davidson represents it, using his own formulation of the principles. How is it that the distinction of 'conditional' and 'unconditional' practical judgments is supposed to eliminate the logical difficulty? How is it that Davidson fails to appreciate the, fairly obvious, point developed above? Even if P1,P2, and D do not formally contradict one another, does it not seem that they are, at least, inconsistent--that they entail a contradiction? For is it not precisely the purpose of considering all things to <u>transform</u> a conditional, or <u>prima facie</u>, judgment <u>into</u> an unconditional one?

Davidson claims that the three theses are not inconsistent--do not entail a contradiction--precisely because, on logical grounds, a consideration of all things does not turn a <u>prima facie</u> judgment into a categorical one. The logic of this move, however, has eluded many, and is, I have argued, mistaken. I think that we can explain Davidson's move, and reinforce the sense that it <u>is</u> an error, by focusing on Davidson's use of the analogy with probabilistic reasoning itself. Secondly, he presses at least two features of probabilistic reasoning which are not in fact mirrored in practical reasoning.

First the misrepresentation. Davidson claims that 'pr' and 'pf' operators insulate statements governed by them from conflicting logically with certain other probabilistic and <u>prima facie</u> statements, and with statements not governed by these operators. It is the alleged lack of conflict with the corresponding 'categorical' statement that is relevant here.

It seems quite false that <u>no</u> probabilistic judgment can conflict logically with a categorical one. "Probably it will rain, because the skies are red" to be sure does not <u>contradict</u> "It will not rain." But let us cease discussing the weather, in regard to which our predictive powers are notoriously imprecise. Rather, imagine a die. We have cast it ten times, marking the top side on each occasion if it is not already marked. After ten throws we have marked six sides. Thus, we know that each of the sides has turned up at least once. On every occasion, the die has turned up '1'. Now, the probability of it turning up '1' on the next throw, based on our evidence, is surely equal to '1'; i.e. pr(the next throw will be a '1', past ten throws and markings)=1, or pr(p,e)=1.

Davidson must claim that this does not logically conflict with the categorical prediction "The die will not be a '1'," i.e. 'not-p'. But this is surely implausible. 'pr(p,e)=1' is not the negation of 'not-p'; but surely the following is a principle (governing non-infinite cases) that would be accepted by any reasonable theory of probability:

B. $[pr(p,e)=1] \rightarrow (e \rightarrow p)$

Thus, by <u>modus ponens</u> twice, we get 'p', which is in flat contradiction to 'not-p'. Probabilistic judgments, where pr=1, do seem to logically conflict with categorical predictions of contrary states of affairs. Contra Davidson and Hempel,[1] it seems eminently reasonable to allow 'detachment' via our plausible principle B, in the limiting case where pr=1. Does it not seem that a practical judgment all things considered is similarly a limiting case? Does it not seem that the practical judgment "I ought to stay in bed, all things considered" similarly entails "I ought to stay in bed" and thus flatly contradicts "I ought to rise and brush," the unconditional judgment attributed in P2?

Davidson might accept the argument regarding probabilistic judgments where pr=1 and yet resist the application to the account of akrasia. Indeed, it may seem that this very point offers him a line of defense regarding akrasia that he had not articulated before. He might reply that it is simply not plausible to construe a practical judgment, all things considered, as analagous to the limiting case in probability,

---

[1] Hempel, <u>Scientific Explanation</u>, p. 379.

where pr=1. Even if we are right that there is a logical conflict in such a case, it does not follow that there is conflict between P1,P2, and D. A practical judgment, all things considered, is not similarly a limiting case, warranting detachment and categorical assertion.

To sharpen Davidson's defense let us distinguish three interpretations of 'pr'and 'pf' statements:

C. pr(p,e)  1. where 'e' is all the evidence there is and could be
2. where 'e' is all the evidence we have available
3. where 'e' is some of the evidence we have available

D. pf(p,e)  1. where 'e' is all the reason there is or could be
2. where 'e' is all the reasons we have available
3. where 'e' is some of the reasons we have available

In both C and D we may take interpretation 1 as characterizing the limiting case where pr=1. Inference to a categorical statement is warranted via principle B. Exceptions to this are rare: e.g. in cases of radioactive decay and quantum physics, for 'pr' statements, and some theory of 'indecidability in principle' in practical reason.[1] I propose to set aside such cases.

Now, in the case of the dies, we know that, on interpretation 2, pr(p,e)=1 because we know that C2=C1, and that pr(p,e)=1 on interpretation 1. Interpretation 1 represents objective or 'metaphysical' probability. Marking the die has provided us with non-probilistic evidence that all the evidence there is and could be is in and that it supports a categorical prediction that the next throw will be a '1'. We are entitled to be 'subjectively certain', and to make a categorical prediction, because

---

[1] Thomas Nagel has set out such a theory in "War and Massacre," <u>Philosophy</u> <u>and</u> <u>Public</u> <u>Affairs</u>, Vol. I, No. 2, (Winter 1972), pp. 123-144.

it is known to be objectively certain that the die will be a '1'.

The case of the akrates, however, and an 'all things considered judgment' is different. Here we do not know that D2=D1. Indeed, there is in general good reason to think that it does not. Given the complexity of practical matters, our limited powers of foresight, insight, etc., it is doubtful that D2 would ever be equal to D1. Since most persons recognize these factors, it is doubtful that they ever _believe_ that D2=D1. Thus, a practical judgment, all things considered, must _remain_ conditional on the reasons specified, in a way that the prediction of the die need not remain conditional on the probabilistic evidence. In the case of practical judgments, detachment is not permitted, via principle B, because no actual practical judgment would satisfy the antecedent. Thus practical judgments 'all things considered' remain _prima facie_, and do not entail a contradiction with the corresponding categorical judgment.

Davidson might strengthen his defense by pointing to a further disanalogy between the limiting case in probability, where pr=1, and practical judgments 'all things considered'. Consider the relation between C2 and C3, and that between D2 and D3. Call all the relevant evidence 'e'; call only some subset of all the evidence 'r'. Now consider the relation between pr(p,e) and pr(not-p,r) on the one hand, and the relation between pf(p,e) and pf(not-p,r) on the other.

Now, pr(p,e) does not logically conflict with pr(not-p,r). Nor does the latter conflict with a categorical prediction of p. However, in general, pr(not-p,r) is of _no interest_ if we know pr(p,e), or if a categorical prediction is warranted. There is a logical compatibility between the statements, but there is a practical incompatibility in asserting both pr(not-p,r) and pr(p,e). Such an assertion would be worse than uninteresting; it would violate what Hempel calls a "maxim for the application of inductive logic," viz. maximal specificity of the reference class. Carnap expresses this "requirement of total evidence" clearly:

> In the application of inductive logic to a given knowledge situation, the total evidence available must be taken as basis for determining the degree of confirmation.[1]

We may, in passing, correct Davidson's own carelessness on this matter. It is not the case that, for example, in a situation of red skies and falling barometers, we may "be equally justified in arguing" that it will rain (with a probability of x) and it will not rain (with a probability of y).[2] The probability of rain, in such a case, is an entirely separate function from the probability of rain given only one, or given only the other. Davidson has (briefly) fallen prey to the very confusion he twits Hare for;[3] he has confounded the making of a judgment with its content or meaning. The content of pr(rain, b) is logically compatible with the content of pr(not-rain, s); but we are certainly not warranted in asserting both. The only assertion to which we are entitled

---

[1] Rudolph Carnap, Logical Foundations of Probability, (Chicago: University of Chicago Press, 1950), cited in Hempel, Scientific Explanation pp. 397-8.

[2] Davidson, "Weakness of Will", p. 108.

[3] Ibid., p. 98.

must take account of all the relevant evidence.

This feature is not mirrored in practical reasoning. There is no practical incompatibility in asserting both pf(p,e) and pf(not-p,r). We have violated no maxim for the application of practical reason should we do so. Indeed, pf(not-p,r) may be of great practical interest even when we know pf(p,e). Even if we judge that 'A is the thing to do, all things considered' it may still be of great importance to recognize that "There is still this to be said against A--it involves breaking my word to Lavinia." One's attitude toward doing A may be affected, and the latter judgment may even have practical consequences--e.g. I may owe Lavinia an explanation and perhaps some compensation.

Davidson's solution to the problem of incontinence cannot be salvaged in this fashion. We have clarified some disanalogies between probabilistic and practical reasoning, between plausible uses of the 'pr' and 'pf' operators. The disanalogies do not, however, substantiate Davidson's claim that P1,P2, and D are compatible. They do not show that there is, in practical reason, a reasonable <u>sharp</u> division between practicle judgments 'all things considered' and 'categorical' practical judgments. Rather, they point the way to <u>further</u> disanalogies. These further differences are quite fatal to Davidson's argument. He tries to exploit precisely those points at which the analogy fails.

A practical judgment 'all things considered' is in fact <u>like</u> an 'unconditional' practical judgment in the theoretically important respects. In order to make such a connection it is not necessary that the reasons the agent has available be all the reasons there are or could be, D2 does not need to be equivalent to D1, nor need the agent believe that they are. If this is how an 'unconditional judgment' were to be understood we could never attribute one to an agent; but there seems to be something right in Davidson's claim that action is geared to unconditional judgments. (We have yet to see exactly what is right here.) In practical reason, the appropriate interpretation of an 'unconditional' judgment surely requires only that the judgment be 'subjectively reasonable' and not 'objectively reasonable'. That is, all that we require is that the action be (judged to be) reasonable in the light of all the reasons the agent has available. The reason for this is straightforward once we reflect on the purposes of probabilistic and practical reasoning respectively.

Probabilistic reasoning is <u>characteristically</u> (but not solely) useful when we have no way of making categorical predictions. We have good reason to think that all the relevant evidence we have still falls short of all the evidence there is or could be. Thus, we characteristically believe that we are <u>not</u> warranted in making a categorical prediction; characteristically we believe that $pr(p,e) \cdot 1$. Certainly this is the case in Davidson's example of predicting the weather. Here we probably believe that our evidence is a causal factor, but we do not know the description under which it would figure in a causal law. Probably red skies, and no rain have a common cause; falling barometers and rain have a common cause; in neither case do we know what the cause is. When one makes a probabilistic prediction, one as it were refuses to commit oneself as to what will 'really' happen; this is prudent, for one often has good reason to think that one does not have ample evidence to make any such rash, categorical, prediction.

*Prima facie* practical judgments, in the ordinary sense of the term, are characteristically parallel in this respect. They contain a similar epistemic reservation. If one says "Doing A is *prima facie* good, because I enjoy it," one is not thereby committed to asserting that it is 'really' good. It is this characteristic of *prima facie* judgments which makes the analogy with probabilistic reasoning attractive in the first place. Moreover, it is this characteristic which explains the fact that *prima facie* judgments recommending contrary actions are not incompatible.

However, a practical judgment 'all things considered' does not normally contain such an epistemic reservation. One may acknowledge that there may be reasons, objectively, that one has not taken into account; but it is not the case that one believes that the reasons one has available do not warrant an unconditional (i.e. unqualified) judgment. Considering all the reasons is precisely how we normally come to an unconditional decision about what is to be done; or, at least, that's as close to an unconditional judgment as we ever get. One is thereby committed to asserting that (so far as one can tell) it is 'really' the correct thing to do. A practical judgment all things considered is not asserted conditionally, with reservations.

In order to emphasize Davidson's mistake here consider a case which fits his description. There are such cases, but they are surely not the norm. We need a case where a person judges that 'a is better than b, all things considered, but also makes this judgment with the epistemic reservation characteristic of probabilistic predictions (where pr<1). It would have to be a case like the following: the person judges that a is better than b, for reasons r1...rn. R1...rn are all the reasons this person has available. The person, however, does not believe that they are all the reasons available; indeed, she/he believes that she/he has perhaps failed to think of some important consideration. Thus, the person does not regard r1...rn under the description 'all things considered' even though r1...rn are in fact 'all things considered'; rather, the person believes that r1...rn are not all the relevant considerations.

It would be possible to read Davidson's D in this fashion, and thus to grant him this formal point. In D it is unspecified whether the agent judges 'a is better than b, all things considered' <u>under that description</u>. (This vagueness parallels Davidson's vagueness about the description under which the akratic act is intentional, c.f. Chapter I, p. 27.) Thus, it is just possible to construe the all things considered judgment as governed by the 'pf' operator in the normal sense of '<u>prima facie</u>,' i.e. the sense in which it indicates a judgment made with epistemic reservations.

It would be possible, but it would be unwise. Aristotle has clearly undermined attempts of this sort to explain away akrasia. (c.f. Chapter V) This would be a person who is 'unsure' or 'vacillating' as to the best thing to do; such a person is not an akrates. <u>Ex hypothesi</u>, the akrates has judged, with no reservations, that the akratic act is not to be done. Davidson himself has emphasized that our account of akrasia will not solve the 'central difficulty' if we resort to moves such as this, where it is appropriate both to apply (under one description) and to withhold (under another description) a given mental predicate.[1]

The crucial blunder, then, is to press the analogy with probabilistic statements too far. Both probabilistic and practical statements are asserted relative to a certain 'ground'--evidence in the one case, reasons in the other. For most probabilistic statements, and for some practical ones, the ground is such that one has good reason to make the assertion only with a certain epistemic reservation. This is not the case, however, with practical judgments based on all the reasons. It is only by supposing that it is the case, even here, that one might plausibly feel the need for another, quite separate practical judgment ('unconditional', 'sans phrase') if "reason is to be practical in its issue and not merely in its subject matter." And, we have found independent reason to reject such an implausible, and unneeded, multiplication of judgments.

Davidson performs this sleight of hand deftly. He draws now on one, now on another, feature of probabilistic reasoning. His introducduction of the (technical) prima facie operator is unexceptionable:

> The concept of prima facie, as it is needed in moral philosophy, relates propositions. In logical grammar 'prima facie' is not an operator on single sentences, much less on predicates of action, but on pairs of sentences related as expressing moral judgment and ground.[2]

---

[1] Ibid., p. 100.   [2] Ibid., p. 109.

He then proceeds to treat the behaviour of the _prima facie_ operator as isomorphic to the behaviour of the probabilistic operator--rather than merely analagous, which is all it plausibly is. This enables him to slide neatly from the claim that if a judgment is _prima facie_, or probabilistic, then it is essentially related to a certain ground--via the fallacy of affirming the consequent--to the claim that if a judgment is related to a certain ground, then that judgment is always governed by the _prima facie_, or probabilistic, operator. If p then q; q; therefore p. Some practical judgments are so governed; some are not. A practical judgment based on all the reasons shares some, but not all features of probabilistic judgments: it is essentially related to a certain ground, it is not plausibly asserted with any epistemic reservations.

Davidson is, of course, entitled to introduce a new and technical use of '_prima facie_' in the discussion of practical reason--one isomorphic to the probability operator and not merely (fallibly) analagous to it. Perhaps it would be more charitable to interpret him as doing just that. But if that is his intent, he needs to demonstrate that it is this _new_ sense of _prima facie_, rather than the normal one, which is in fact 'needed in moral philosophy', and in the analysis of _all_ practical judgments based on reasons. This he does not do. Rather, he exploits some associations of the normal term which indicate he could not do so successfully--in particular the epistemic reservations so characteristic of ordinary _prima facie_ judgments.

We have located one theoretically significant disanalogy between practical reasoning and probabilistic reasoning. There is a second: the analysis of a judgment all things considered. Had Davidson recognized that the two models diverge in at least _this_ respect, he might have avoided one highly implausible thesis which does not even advance his case. Pressing, again, his analogy too far, he concludes "We have no clue how to arrive at [(the all things considered judgment)] from the reasons." A legitimate astonishment at this is brushed off with the observation ". . . but in this respect moral reasoning is no worse off than predicting the weather,"[1] and "it's faulty prototype [in theory A] was in no better shape."[2] Theory A was in no better shape, but it was in no worse shape either. The inability of theory A to account for the fact that we weigh and balance various, sometimes conflicting, considerations was found, earlier, to be a serious flaw. Surely this lacuna in Davidson's account is serious as well. And there is no need for it. All that's required is to bear in mind that analogy is different from isomorphism.

It is true that (most) empirical probability statements based on all the evidence are not derived _at all_ from any weighting of the various independent probabilities, based on individual pieces of evidence.[3] In the case of the weather, however, a prediction based on all the evidence is an entirely separate function from a prediction based only on red

---

[1] Ibid., p. 109.   [2] Ibid., p. 110.

[3] The most striking exception to this, of course, are certain statistical uses of probability, where we _know_ that the variables are independent. In such cases there are formula to apply, contra Davidson.

skies, or only on falling barometers. In a situation where we have both conditions, the appropriate function hovers, notoriously, around .5. Davidson, therefore, gives up any attempt to characterize practical reasoning as arriving at a reasoned decision as to what to do. But surely practical reasoning is far better off than predicting the weather in this respect, and probably worse off than certain statistical uses of probability, where the variables are independent.

But this is implausible, and not required. It seems in general true that if the considerations for doing A are insignificant or minimal, while the considerations against are held to be very important, we do conclude, <u>on this basis</u>, that the act is not to be done. We do not, of course, have a "general formula" to apply to such considerations; if we did the want theorist would be in better shape than she/he is. Nonetheless, we are often able to make such comparisons of significance, and the conclusion seems to be the <u>result</u> of the comparison. Aristotle, for example, provides an account of practical reason, which provides a perfectly cogent account of this function. (c.f.Chap.V below.) It is, to be sure, hard to 'add up' the considerations Davidson provides. That is npt a general argument against such a possibility however. Rather it indicates that these cases are not adequately spelled out.

D. The Weatherman Approach in Perspective

For all the reasons discussed above, I think that Davidson fails to demonstrate the compatibility of P1,P2, and the existence of akratic acts in the sense defined. A theoretically significant distinction between practical judgments all things considered and 'unconditional' judgments cannot be sustained. There is no good reason to think that one is any less, nor any more, 'practical in its issue' than the other. This accounts for our original intuition that, even if the logical sleight-of-hand could be sustained, the inconsistency would simply come up again, if we used slightly revised, but no less plausible, principles or definition of akrasia. And, of course, this failure eliminates any motivation to force, implausibly, an 'unconditional judgment' that the akratic act is <u>better</u> on the akrates.

I think it is doubtful that even Davidson consistently thinks that his principles are compatible:

> For how is it possible for a man to judge that a is better than b, all things considered, and not judge that a is better than b? One potential confusion is quickly set aside. 'a is better than b, all things . . . considered' surely does entail 'a is better than b', <u>and we do not want to explain incontinence as a simple logical blunder</u> . . . Setting this straight, however, seems only to emphasize the real difficulty.[1] (emphasis mine)

Indeed it seems to. Davidson is apparently willing to grant the very conclusions we have reached, 'quickly' setting aside a 'confusion' which followed naturally from his earlier remarks, and which took some doing to sort out.

When Davidson addresses himself to what he now takes to be the 'real difficulty' he gives up further reference to 'unconditional' judgments, or practical judgments <u>sans phrase</u> in any explanatory role. In what is apparently the heart of his account he seems even to jettison any of the

---

[1] Ibid., p. 110.

distinctions we have been considering, at his bidding. He no longer distinguishes prima facie judgments (in the normal sense of the term), judgments all things considered, and unconditional judgments at all. "Every judgment," he says, "is made in the light of all the reasons."[1] Thus, despite the emphasis he elsewhere places on the conditional/unconditional distinction, I propose that we examine his last conclusion, which is formulated without reference to this troublesome notion.

In fact, I think that Davidson's solution turns on a rejection of both P1 and P2.

> There is no paradox in supposing a person sometimes holds that all he believes and values supports a certain course of action, when at the same time those same beliefs and values cause him to reject that course of action.[2]

It seems that the notion Davidson was trying to capture by 'unconditional judgment' and 'practical judgment sans phrase' is simply the cause of the action.

It is generally thought important that the cause of an action involve a judgment of some kind. In the normal case, according to Davidson, the cause of the action is a reason, and a reason contains a judgment as an essential constituent (c.f. "Actions, Reasons, and Causes"). If akrasia is to be a case of intentional action, it too must be caused by a reason, and thereby (in part) by a judgment. However, we have found no way plausibly to attribute the judgment 'a is better than b' together

---

[1] Ibid., p. 111.   [2] Ibid., p. 111.

with the judgment 'b is better than a, all things considered.'[1] It seems quite implausible to suggest that the akrates does judge that 'a is better than b;' and even if she/he (on occasion) does, it does not advance the argument. It still seems plausible, however, to attribute the judgment 'b is better than a, all things considered.' Thus, I shall interpret Davidson as claiming that there is no paradox in supposing that the judgment 'b is better than a, all things considered,' causes the agent to do a.

This thesis is connected to a peculiar claim noted earlier, and re-emphasized and strengthened by Davidson here. This is the claim that there are no discernible regularities connecting reasons and a reasoned conclusion.

> Every judgment is made in the light of all the reasons . . . but this does not mean that every judgment is reasonable, or thought to be so by the agent, on the basis of those reasons, nor that the judgment be reached from that basis by a process of reasoning . . . If r is someone's reason for holding that p, then his holding that r must be, I think, a cause of his holding that p. But, and this is what is crucial here, his holding that r may cause his holding that p . . . [even if] the agent thinks that r is a reason to reject p.[2]

Thus, the claim is the following: a reason r may cause a judgment p, even though the agent believes that, in view of r, it is unreasonable to judge p; and a judgment p may cause an action a even though the agent believes that a is unreasonable in the light of the judgment that caused it. According to Davidson there is nothing paradoxical in either case.

---

[1] Grice concurs, though on the basis of a different argument.

[2] Ibid., p. 111.

1. **Token materialism and the anomaly of the mental**

To suppose that it is paradoxical is to fail to appreciate two other of Davidson's doctrines--viz. token materialism and the anomaly of the mental.[1] Token materialism is a claim of extreme and deliberate weakness on the relation of the mental and the physical in general, of reasons and actions as one instance. The anomalousness of the mental makes it prudent to accept no stronger thesis here. The latter doctrine asserts that there are no laws connecting mental events either with other mental events or with physical events. Ipso facto there are no laws connecting reasons and actions so described. If the mental is anomalous, and if materialism is true, it follows that only token, and not type identities will be forthcoming. Telling the truth is caused by brain state b1 today, b2 tomorrow, and b50 next week, even though I may have done it for the same reason in each case.

How are we to understand action explanations in this scheme? Davidson asserts that there are no laws connecting reasons and actions so described; still, he is loathe to give up the traditional view that "explanations 'involve laws.'"[2] The solution--ingenious and elegant--is to suggest that the token events that are the having of a reason and the action do satisfy a covering law, but only under some redescription. The law itself, in all probability, will deal not with the concepts

---

[1] The clearest statement of these views is in "Mental Events," in Experience and Theory, pp. 79-102. Parts of the doctrine also figure importantly in Davidson, "Actions."

[2] Davidson, "Actions," p. 194.

'reason' and 'action', but with classifications which are "neurological, chemical, or physical."[1] Moreover, the laws appropriate to many instances of "telling the truth because it is my duty" may well not even overlap. What warrants our acceptance of reasons *as* *explanations* of action is our faith (for it is surely no more than that) that particular instances of reason and action are grounded in *some* (probably micro) covering law.

To return to the case at hand. One consequence of these two doctrines is the reasonable expectation that causal relations will be not isomorphic with logical relations. That is, the causal relations between noting reasons, forming a practical conclusion, and acting on it will not always map neatly onto the logical relations between conclusion and *good* (or sufficient) reasons and between concluding practically and acting *in* *accord* *with* that conclusion. To invoke once again Davidson's useful distinction: causal relations obtain between *the* *making* of judgments and acting, logical relations between *the* *content* of judgments, and the evaluation of actions.

P1 and P2, of course, appear to assert a kind of correspondence between causal relations and logical relations that is here denied on principle. And there is something paradoxical about the claim that sometimes the nexus of reasons cause action A, sometimes action not-A, and that nothing more can be said philosophically about this surprising fact. One expects that, if reasons are a kind of cause, then, at least normally, the reasons one adduces in support of action A tend to cause A--

---

[1]Ibid., p. 195.

not not-A. Still, it is surely possible to imagine cases where they do diverge. It is not common to find causal connections and rational connections sharply divergent, but it happens. And if it happens, why cannot open-eyed akrasia be admitted, as a member of this class?

Consider some familiar examples. The American Cancer Society sponsors some of the most tasteful and effective advertising on American television. They provide persuasive arguments, and vivid situations, which really 'drive home' the fact that smoking is an utterly irrational practice. Invariably, the ads evoke such judgments from the smokers present; and just as invariably they immediately light up a cigarette. The judgment may well seem to cause the very act that it proscribes. This phenomenon is common with the more fleshly forms of akrasia. The dieter's discussion of the harms and distastfulness of chocolate eclairs can swiftly cause an intense longing for one, and sometimes a headlong rush for the patisserie. The most sincere of discussions as to the inadvisability of an affair can inflame the passions and catapult a couple into bed. Whether the judgment be for or against, its very entertainment brings the subject to mind, activates the emotions, and, it seems, can cause action. These seem to be clear cases where a judgment which fails to rationalize x nonetheless causes (or is at least part of the cause of) the doing of x.

## 2. Criticism of the account and the perspective

If this is in fact Davidson's account of akrasia it falls very far short of the account we had reason to expect. First, it is at least inadequate because it is insufficiently detailed. It does not pick out all and only antecedently clear akratic acts; it picks out too much.

Consider the range of events picked out by the condition 'caused by a psychological event which does not rationalize the physical event.' Members of this class would include not only cases of akrasia (if indeed, akrasia is a member); it would also include a wide range of other events which are clearly not cases of akrasia. It would include the more bizarre exploits reported of persons tripping on acid--e.g. "I leapt from the roof because I believed (due to the acid) that I could fly." It would include the writhings of heart attack victims, when the attack is precipitated, e.g. by a fit of rage. And it would include those epileptic gyrations of Dostoyevsky, when the seizure was caused by an emotional state. Clearly, to be an account of akrasia we need an account which is, at least, _more specific_ than this. The akrates, unlike these other types, has at least _a reason_ for what she/he does.

But the trouble runs deeper than this. Akrasia cannot be _at all_ the kind of macro failure that Davidson here locates. Akrasia is not even a member of this broad and amorphous class of breakdowns. Members of this class are not cases of intentional action; _ipso facto_ akrasia is not amongst them. Akrasia is defined as a case of intentional action.

The reason for this is straightforward. In order to be an intentional act, it is not sufficient that an act be caused by beliefs and desires. It must be caused by beliefs and desires which _rationalize_ the act, i.e. beliefs and desires which "lead us to see something the agent prized, held dear . . . thought beneficial."[1] But the beliefs and desires which cause the akratic act, according to this account, do not rationalize it. Indeed they proscribe it. Consequently, the act cannot be intentional under the 'all things considered' description.

Nor is it intentional under any other description for it is not caused by any other beliefs and desires. To be sure, the act is rationalized by some subset of the agent's beliefs and desires--say, a judgment some things considered. It is this subset of beliefs and desires which the skeptic emphasizes. But Davidson has insisted, against the skeptic, that there need be no dislocation of the agent's total belief system. Davidson insists that we must account for the case where the akrates has an "unclouded, unwavering judgment" that the act is not for the best, and yet performs it intentionally. An account which required that only a subset of beliefs and desires were operative would be like the Aristotelian skeptic's in precisely the way that Davidson has rejected.[2]

Thus, Davidson's account provides not even the appearance of an explanation. He concludes, unilluminatingly, that "akrasia is essentially surd."[3] But we knew that at the beginning. The trouble with the account is that akrasia must satisfy a macro generalization--it must be rationalized by its cause--if it is to be intentional; but it is precisely

---

[1] Ibid., p. 179.

[2] This point is discussed further below, p. 176.

[3] Ibid., p. 113.

defined so as to be unable to satisfy such a generalization--one acts despite the fact that one's reasons all things considered proscribe it. One acts on <u>a</u> reason, but acknowledges that that reason has been overridden by others more weighty.

This trouble may be obscured from Davidson himself because of certain features of token materialism and the doctrine of the anomalousness of the mental. These very features, however, are troublesome in their own right. To recap briefly: the token materialist suspects that there are no laws connecting reasons and actions so described, yet is loathe to give up the traditional view that "explanations 'involve laws.' Thus, the claim is that reasons explain, when they do, not because of any regularities they exhibit under that description. Rather, reasons explain because we believe that there is some <u>other</u> true description-- probably "neurological, chemical, or physical"--which applies to each particular case, and which does instantiate a law.

Thus, it is not in virtue of any of the <u>differentia</u> of rationalization that reasons explain actions. Rather it is solely in virtue of belonging to the species 'causal explanation.' <u>Qua</u> rationalization, reason explanations "serve a different function" from that of being a "predictive law in the rough"; they "provide evidence for the existence of a causal law governing the case at hand."[1] The causal law itself will use entirely different terms.

Explanation, as it were, proceeds <u>through</u> law--like connections

---

[1] Davidson, "Actions," p. 193-4.

at the micro level. A reason explains an action because, and only because, we believe it to be identical with a neurological, chemical, or physical state or event; that event, in turn, is connected in a law-like way with another neurological, chemical, or physical state or event; and the latter event is identical to the action. There is nothing about the macro level _itself_ which makes mention of items in its terms explanatory. Reasons and action so described, fail to exhibit the regularities required for explanation. Thus, reasons explain actions only via connection to causal explanation at the micro level; they 'provide evidence for' the existence of respectable laws, at quite a different level, using quite different terms.

Against this background, it is easy to see why Davidson reminds us that akrasia is "essentially surd", that is, is not rationalized by its cause. But it is not easy to see why he thinks the "actor cannot understand himself", nor, by extrapolation, that we cannot understand the actor. "Reading reason into behaviour" is at best an accidental feature of explanation in the _normal_ case of explanation. It is not anything about rationalization _per se_ which ever provides the explanation of an act. The macro level itself is not where explanation ever proceeds. If rationalization is not central to the explanation in the normal case, it is surely no more so in the case of akrasia.

These features of the general theory, however, are unwelcome. First, they tempt us to ignore the quite central fact that akrasia is intentional. Second, they make it mysterious that the category of

<u>intentional</u> action generally should have, for us, the importance that it does. Intentionality has macro criteria -- rationalization by the cause -- but the force of the general theory is precisely to pare down the explanatory significance of macro terms. Third, the general theory, with its extreme and deliberate weakness is surely a view of the very last resort. If any stronger thesis were tenable, it would be preferable, simply because it says <u>more</u>. It is at least not obvious that reasons and actions are <u>as</u> anomalous as Davidson claims; this claim warrants examination. Most seriously, the general view assumes a highly implausible account of explanation -- viz. that explanation is transparent. That is, it assumes that if a explains b under particular descriptions, then any other true description of a will also explain any other true description of b. Davidson has forcefully reminded us that causality is transparent; but causal explanation surely is not.

### E. Summary So Far

We have considered, and found to be wanting, two proposed accounts of open-eyed akrasia. Thus, we are not yet in a position to answer in the affirmative Davidson's question ,"Does it never happen that I have an unclouded, unwavering judgment that my action is not for the best, and yet perform it"', as an act of akrasia. We have not justified Davidson's confidence, shared by many, that "it seems absolutely certain that it does" because we have not yet found an account of open-eyed akrasia which is compatible with a reasonable general theory of the explanation of action.

Let us review briefly the reasons why neither the want theorist nor Davidson provides an adequate general theory. One important reason for our rejection of their respective accounts of akrasia was the inadequacy of the general theoretical frameworks. In order to produce a better account of akrasia, we will need to do so within a better theoretical framework.

The want-theorist's account of open-eyed akrasia -- surely the most intuitively attractive -- was compatible with a general covering law theory like Goldman's. However, the explanations provided by that theory were argued to be either false or vacuous. Thus, the theory foundered on the familiar shoals of Scylla and Charybdis. Either the required antecedent conditions simply did not obtain, or such falsification was avoided by giving up any reasonably complete independent checks on the presence of the antecedent. Since the explanations of all actions, within this scheme, are either false or vacuous, so is the explanation in the special case of akrasia. This point holds despite the intuitive attraction of the account. This flaw was highlighted by noting that the want theorist simply transforms a problem in accounting for akrasia into an equal and opposite problem in accounting for continence. Indeed, after pressing these arguments against the general theory, the account even of akrasia lost some of its initial attraction, at least for quite a range of cases of akrasia.

Davidson's account of open-eyed akrasia holds little intuitive attraction. It seems highly implausible to attribute to the akrates an 'unconditional judgment' that the akratic act is better than refraining, together with a judgment, based on all the reasons, that refraining is better than acting akratically. The general theory -- the Weatherman approach -- offered to support this part of the account of akrasia, depends upon a radical separation of practical reasoning, on the one hand, and 'unconditional' practical judgments, and actions, on the other. Davidson, however, fails to offer good reasons for accepting this curious view. The reason, I have argued, that he does not take more care to defend this part of the account is that his real interest lies elsewhere. It is, in fact, his quite separate doctrines of token materialism and the anomalousness of the mental that carry the real weight of the argument.

Now token materialism is, in all probability, neither false nor vacuous. To this extent, Davidson's general theory is superior to Goldman's. Token materialism is doubtless true; but this is because it is enormously weak. Davidson, and others, espouse it because of doubts that true and interesting covering laws obtain, in general, at the macro level of explanation -- the level which mentions reasons and actions. Belief in the anomalousness of the mental is one, but only one, reason for believing token materialism. However, when Davidson abandons the macro level of explanation in his account of akrasia, the account simply disintegrates. At this point the account becomes insufficiently detailed to distinguish akrasia from other failures of macro regularities such as psychotic breaks, epileptic fits, and the writhings of heart attack victims, when these events are caused by certain kinds of psychological states. Worse, akrasia cannot even be the kind of macro failure that Davidson locates. Members of this class are not cases of intentional action; *ipso facto* akrasia is not amongst them. Akrasia is defined as a case of intentional action. The token materialist tenets upon which Davidson relies here are simply too weak to guarantee this quite central feature to akrasia. Far from providing an account of open-eyed akrasia, certain features of token materialism enable him surreptitiously to change the subject.

Thus two general theories of the explanation of action have been rejected as inadequate, and with them their accounts of open-eyed akrasia. A better general theory is, of course, desirable in its own right, and is necessary if we are to provide an account of akrasia, whether open-eyed or otherwise. I suggest that it will be promising to look for a macro theory -- that is, one mentioning reasons and actions, and not simply neurophysiology. We pre-theoretically believe that some regularities do obtain at this level, that the mental is not all that anomalous. And, it seems that we cannot simply abandon the macro level while yet preserving the quite central feature of intentionality, both for action in general and for akrasia in particular.

The traditional view is widely accepted that explanations require a certain sort of regularity in the phenomenon to be explained.[1] If macro explanations are to be possible, there must be some kind of macro regularities to which we can appeal. But what kind? The failure of Goldman's account is the failure of the best extant attempt to set out regularities connecting action with its psychological antecedents in a

---

[1] c.f., Chapter II, p. 59.

law-like fashion. Perhaps a better account of this sort will be forthcoming. At this point, however, I suggest that it will be more fruitful to turn in a different direction. I propose that we follow up Davidson's suggestion that generalizations like those connecting reasons and actions serve a 'different function' from that sort of covering law connecting action and antecedents.[1] It will be prudent, however, to take that suggestion in a different direction than he does himself.

I turn now to sketching out a theory of the explanation of action which is a macro theory -- that is, it traces out regularities between reasons and actions <u>so described</u>. It is a theory which is, I believe, to be found in Aristotle. It is stronger, more ambitious, than Davidson's token materialism, and the 'non-theory' of the anomalousness of the mental. It is also a theory which is, I believe, neither false nor vacuous; thus, it escapes the unhappy fate of the want theorist. Finally, with this good general theory before us, we may turn to consider the possibility, or lack thereof, of accounting for open-eyed akrasia within the terms of that theory. If it is compatible with this theory, well and good; Davidson's challenge will have been answered. If it is not compatible, the burden of proof will have been shifted from the skeptics to the believers.

---

[1] Davidson, "Actions", p. 193.

CHAPTER IV

TELEOLOGICAL EXPLANATION

A.  Back to the Data

Let us begin this fresh attempt to exhibit the structure of action explanation by considering a concrete instance. The explanation of one action is successful; the (very similar) explanation of another is not. This contrast is useful in focusing the kinds of regularities, or generalizations, which are in fact essential to action explanation. That is, what connections are present in an explanation which works, and absent in an explanation which doesn't. It is plausible that these will be the connections which are required for action explanation generally.

Let us return to Henry and Madeline. He has, you remember, insulted her, and she demands an explanation. She wants to know the reasons for his act. Because, he replies, she has tarnished his honor by asking him publicly whether he lied to the Senate Committee about his role in wire taps on subordinates. "But you are a politician", she replies; politicians have been known to lie before; it is important that they be held accountable for their statements, fair that they be questioned when there is evidence that they have lied. No, he is not a politician, Henry counters. He is a statesman, and above such petty matters. She, and the rest of the press, ought to know that. He is an honorable man, and he will resign if she, and her collegues, do not retract their disgraceful innuendos. But more immediately, his insult is an appropriate response to her crude tactics.

I think that Henry has successfully explained both his insult and his outrage. We understand his action by placing it against a complex and systemmatic background of other factors not explicitly mentioned. That background includes most importantly certain beliefs and goals that we reasonably attribute to Henry. We know that Henry views himself in a particular social context, that he knows, values, and observes certain social conventions characteristic of that context. An appeal to 'honor' in the American political scene generally is rather anomalous; however, we know that Henry views himself as part of quite another, more noble, order, viz., that of statesman (We may even know that he wrote a dissertation on statesmanship, not politics). If we are acquainted with this social context, we would expect 'honor' to matter to Henry; a broad range of his other activities are best explained by supposing that he does; and we would understand why Henry believes that he is required to 'defend' it here. Defending his honor is more important to him than possibly alienating the press further, or appearing foolish to politicians, like Hubert, who do not understand these conventions. Our, and Henry's, understanding of social practices that are part of codes of honor also explain why Henry's remark was an insult rather than an explitive; he is an elite European, not a _nouveau riche_ Texas cowboy. It is our understanding of _Henry's view_ of these matters that is crucial to the explanation. We need not, of course, share these views ourselves.

The heart of the contextual background, then, consists in our expectations about Henry's behavior, based upon our beliefs about his beliefs and goals. The crucial role of this background in the explanation can be emphasized by contrasting the adequacy of this explanation, offered by Henry, with its patent inadequacy, were it to be offered by Ron.

Ron has long been well known to be a rather seedy character. He is frequently suspected of lying to the press, and sometimes asked about it. "Ron, last week you said p, this week you say not-p. Have you changed your mind or just your story?" Ron has always replied simply, "The previous story is inoperative." When pressed further, he has sometimes expressed annoyance, sometimes even anger. Today, however, he appears indignant, insults the press, and claims that his honor has been tarnished. The natural reply, of course, is "Your honor! You've never minded about that before! Whatever do you mean?" A natural further question would be to wonder how he could have acquired the capacity to make such a sophisticated response as an insult. Neither the insult, nor the explanation 'fit' with what we know about Ron.

Nothing in his previous behaviour suggests that he either knows or cares about codes of honor. Indeed, everything in his previous behaviour suggests that he cares most about goals quite incompatible with what 'honor' would dictate. Given the system of beliefs and goals that it is reasonable to <u>attribute to Ron</u>, the proffered explanation simply does not work. The reason appealed to has no reasonable place amongst Ron's aims, pursuits, or values.

One might usefully introduce the term 'psychological system' to refer to the beliefs and goals it is reasonable to attribute to individual persons. The systems of Henry and Ron diverge over the place, and lack thereof, of honor within them. (They coincide, no doubt, at numerous other points, such as the place of survival needs and perhaps even [personal] love and achievement). The precise structuring of psychological systems is no doubt rather loose. Should Henry have to choose between preserving his honor and survival, the outcome might be unclear.

(And, as Anscombe remarks, some of the goals of some reasonable persons may be both incompatible and incommensurable -- how would one order the sacrifice of the Mona Lisa, set against the sacrifice of a newborn child?) Still, there are many clear orders of priority; honor is a goal we attribute to Henry, and it clearly takes precedence over others, that we also attribute to him, such as keeping harmony with the press, and not being mocked by Hubert. Hierarchical relations between goals are an important factor in creating a system out of the multiplicity of an individual's pursuits.

A certain pattern of action explanation emerges clearly from these two cases. As was desired, the terms appealed to are macro terms -- they involve reasons and actions and other general psychological facts about persons, rather than the terms of neurophysiology, chemistry and physics. A reason seems to explain an action, when it does, by providing a certain sort of description of the act. The explanation succeeds when the action, under that description, can be related in some systemmatic way to the aims, goals and characteristic activities of the particular agent.

The relation of action and reasons is roughly that of means to ends. The reason describes the end toward which the action can be seen to be a means. Henry's insult is seen to be a reasonable means to the end of preserving his honor. Had he uttered an explitive, by contrast, it would not have been a reasonable means to that end. Indeed it would conflict with honor codes. An explitive, had Henry uttered it, would not yet be explained. Moreover, the action must be related in this way to some goal that it is reasonable to attribute to the particular agent. It is because honor has a coherent place within the psychological system we attribute to Henry that his action was successfully explained. It is because there was no reasonable way to locate 'honor' within the psychological system we attribute to Ron that his action failed to be explained.

From the foregoing it is evident that beliefs and goals are attributed to persons systemmatically on the basis of fairly extensive patterns of behaviour. Rationality on the part of the agent is presupposed -- actions are explained only as (more or less) <u>reasonable</u> means to a particular goal. And the goal must be one that the agent pursues with some kind of regularity. We disallow isolated and <u>ad hoc</u> references to goals in attempted explanations of acts which are isolated and out of character.

> The circularity of these inter-locking specifications [of beliefs and goals] is no accident. Ascriptions of beliefs and desires must be interdependent, and the only points of anchorage are the demonstrable needs for survival, the

regularities of behaviour, and the assumptions, grounded in faith in natural selection, of optimal design.[1]

It is for this reason that we reject Ron's explanation of his insult, and not, for example, because we think he introspected poorly and misidentified the psychological event that caused the act.[2]

The prevalence of, and sometimes necessity for, explanations in terms of further reasons reflects these conditions on successful action explanations. Further reasons are characteristically sought when ones *prima facie* expectations about action are defied. Explanations which provide further reasons exhibit how a particular act is related (appearances to the contrary notwithstanding) to some goal it is reasonable to attribute to the agent. As Dennett remarks, "The demand for reasons for intentional action is not a demand with fixed limits, since there is no fixed length for the nested reasons one must give."[3] Central to the length of 'nested reasons' which are *in fact* sought, and required if a particular action is to be explained, is how many steps are required before the action is placed within a pattern of what are reasonably believed to be the aims characteristic of the particular person whose action is being explained.

These features of action explanation fit naturally with the (possibly diverse) group of explanations generally called teleological.

---

[1] D. C. Dennett, "Intentional Systems", The Journal of Philosophy, Vol. LXVIII, No. 4 (February 25, 1971), p. 93

[2] Most likely, contra Goldman, we have no view on this matter. And in any case, even if Ron did have such a *thought* just prior to action, an appeal to it would still not *explain* the insult.

[3] D. C. Dennett, Content and Consciousness, London: Routledge and Kegan Paul, 1969, p. 170.

And, in fact, there is broad agreement amongst philosophers that the explanation of action is in fact teleological. There is not, however, broad agreement on the nature of teleological explanation. Davidson says:

> It is an error to think that, because placing the action in a larger context explains it, therefore we now understand the sort of explanation involved. Talk of patterns and contexts does not answer the question how reasons explain action.[1]

Many philosophers believe that the teleological explanation of action can be understood only as a species of ordinary causal explanation -- that is, actions are explained when reasons are provided because we cite a psychological antecedent which brings about the action. We have investigated two of the best attempts to date to articulate such a theory -- that of Goldman and that of Davidson. Neither of these accounts, however, is satisfactory.

It is possible, of course, that another, better, causal interpretation may be forthcoming. Such an account is not at present available. And indeed there is little positive reason to insist on an interpretation in ordinary causal terms. Given the problems in philosophical psychology that plague us, it is not surprising that the antecedents of such laws and their instances prove elusive. Those who do argue for an ordinary causal interpretation of action explanation appeal characteristically to 'what else then' arguments.[2] The force of this move is considerably diminished when we are readily able to produce an alternative.

---

[1] Davidson, "Actions", p. 187.

[2] Davidson argues that the explanatory context of cause and effect is one we "understand as well as any"; Berofsky, that it is one at any rate that we "have to understand anyway".

The regularities we have been tracing do not, on the face of them, appeal at all to events or states antecedent to the action, connected in a law-like way with actions of that sort. Rather they appeal to co-temporaneous or future goals -- states of affairs to be brought about by the action. I suggest that the teleological explanation of action is best understood as a species of functional explanation. This is a form of explanation, separate from causal explanation, with a desirable generality that is clearly illuminating. Moreover this interpretation seems better suited to clarify certain central features of action explanation. First, we are able to explain and understand actions even in the ignorance of psychological antecedents (if any) under which we now labor. Functional explanation does not require that we be able to identify 'causes' independently of their 'effects'; thus our inability to do so in explaining actions is not troublesome. Second, it explains the fact that rationality appears to function in reason explanations as a constitutive requirement, and not as an empirical hypothesis. (This interpretation also illuminates the fact that acts are not <u>over determined</u> when the action is explained by a reason; the action is identical to a particular bodily movement, and the bodily movement has a neurological explanation, and there are no type identities between psychological states and neurophysiological states).

## B. Final Causes

Amongst the events, processes and states for which we seek explanation, some of them are, or are parts of, orderly processes that seem goal directed. These are events, processes and states that belong to coherent self-preserving and self-maintaining systems. The intentional action of persons is perhaps the clearest example of such events. There are others. They include the nonintentional normal functioning of plant and animal bodies, and the activities of complex mechanical devices like computers, typewriters, automobiles.

Such systems characteristically succeed in reaching their goals. Their activities are persistent and flexible in the face of obstacles. Should an obstacle to one route to the goal prove insuperable, the system often finds another. For systems of this sort, information about <u>what</u> the goal of a particular orderly process is, or <u>how</u> a particular event contributes to that goal, is frequently felt to provide a kind of information that is illuminating. Such information supplements, it does not supplant, information about what events brought the process about, -- that is, normal causal explanations in terms of antecedents. But functional explanations may be available when a particular (normal) causal account is unknown. As Dennett remarks, the 'tactic' of adopting the 'functional stance' in explanation 'pays off' particularly when "we have reason to suppose the assumption of optimal design is warranted, and doubt the practicality of prediction from...the physical stance."[1] Even when an explanation in terms of antecedents is available, however, functional explanation may well still be of interest.

---

[1] Dennett, "Intentional Systems", pp. 87-106.

The subject matter of functional explanations is characteristically whole systems, organic or otherwise. The terminology of functional explanations characteristically refers to needs, goals, purposes, and to events as 'means to' satisfying a need, reaching a goal, realizing a purpose.

Functional systems vary enormously in the complexity of the behaviour which is apparently goal directed. Most plant behaviour, for example, is relatively simple: its survival needs are for light, air and nourishment; most of its activities contribute straightforwardly and efficiently to the satisfaction of these needs. The goal directed behaviour of persons, by contrast, falls at (or near) the other end of the spectrum of complexity. Persons may travel, or manipulate the environment to acquire food. And they may do so whether or not they actually need to: sometimes we do not recognize foods in the environment, sometimes we do but want some other delicacy.

It is such special complexities in the goal directed behaviour of some teleological systems that lead us to view them as intentional entities. Beliefs and desires may usefully be construed as theoretical entities which we introduce in the explanation of some goal directed behaviour, to account for special complexities it exhibits. Much goal directed behaviour of persons is not directed to any plausible need: attributing psychological states such as desires enables us to proliferate suitable goals in a way required to make functional sense of these activities. Other goal directed behaviour fails to reach any suitable goal: the introduction of beliefs (which, as it happens are mistaken) can enable us to make sense of the activity anyway. Thus, the introduction of psychological states in functional explanation serves at least two theoretically useful purposes. It enables us to apply functional explanation to complex as well as simple goal directed activities. And it enables us to make sense of certain apparently goal-directed activities which do not succeed in reaching any appropriate goal.

Functional explanations are widely agreed to exhibit, at least prima facie, certain 'logical peculiarities', to be, at least prima facie, a 'scientific anomaly'. They have about them a 'flavor of futurity'. According to Scheffler such explanations "apparently refer to the ends of action (events, processes) rather than to its determinants". Hempel characterizes it as a kind of "explanation not by reference to causes which 'bring about' the event in question, but by reference to ends which determine its course". Von Wright focuses the contrast with (so-called) scientific explanation nicely:

> Causal explanation points to the past. 'This happened because that had occurred.' Teleological explanation points to the future. 'This happened in order that that should occur.'[1]

This anomalousness may usefully be articulated in terms of three contrasts with ordinary causal explanations. These contrasts will both exhibit the structure of functional explanation and also explain why this interpretation of action explanation avoids the pitfalls to which ordinary causal interpretations succumb. Each contrast draws out a consequence

---

[1]Scheffler, Inquiry, p. 89; Hempel, Scientific Explanation, p. 303; Von Wright, Explanation and Understanding, p. 83.

of the optimality (rationality) assumption that is fundamental to functional explanation.

A certain difference in the 'form of functional laws' follows naturally from the fact that they do not explain an event in terms of antecedents.

> Qua teleological, these laws will not be of a kind which makes behaviour a function of the state of some [antecedent] 'unobservable entity'; rather the law explains the behaviour as a function of the system and environment; but the relevant feature of the system and environment will [not be its immediately antecedent state, but rather will] be what the condition of both make necessary [or a member of a disjunctive set of necessary conditions] if the end is to be realized.[1]

Functional analysis seeks to "understand a behaviour pattern...by determining the role it plays in keeping the given system in proper working order." More formally:

> The object of the analysis is some item i, which is a relatively persistent trait or disposition occurring in a system s, and the analysis aims to show that when s is in a state or internal condition c1 and in an environment representing certain external conditions ce...cn the trait i has effects which satisfy some need or functional requirement of s, i.e. a condition n which is necessary [or a member of a disjunctive set of necessary conditions] for the system's remaining in adequate, or effective, or proper working order.[2]

Special complexities in the behaviour of functional systems to which we attribute psychological states have already been mentioned. This model applies to the case of the explanation of intentional action in the following way: the object of the analysis, i, is the intentional action. The system, s, is the agent qua psychological system -- that is qua

---

[1] Charles Taylor, Behaviour, p. 9

[2] Hempel, Scientific Explanation, pp. 303, 306.

ordered system of beliefs, goals, characteristic activities. The explanation aims to show that when the agent, s, believes her/himself to be in a state or internal condition $c_1$, and believes her/himself to be in an environment representing certain external conditions $ce...cn$, such that she/he believes that the performance of the action, i, has effects which satisfy (produce, instantiate) a particular goal of s, then the agent does i. Henry's insult to Madeline is explained because we see that he believed himself to be compromised by the (external) circumstance of Madeline's accusation, and he believed that insulting her was one appropriate means of defending his good name.

Persons *qua* practical agents, unlike persons *qua* biological organisms, clearly have a multiplicity of ends. "Adequate, effective, or proper working" is a much more complex matter in the case of intentional systems than in the case of non-intentional ones. It is not, however, unmanagably complex. There is normally available a relatively small set of goals (and beliefs) which enable us to explain a wide range of behaviour with a fair degree of economy. Such economy in explanation is facilitated by the fact that goals tend to be hierarchically ordered, with some taking clear precedence over others. Being mocked by Hubert is something Henry would like to avoid, but it is clearly less important to him than defending his honor. Economy is furthered by the fact that goals are more and less inclusive -- a wide range of 'lower order' ends are often subsumable under one more encompassing. These hierarchical relations amongst ends are expressed in P1.

The optimality assumption itself, and the form of functional laws, guarantee that there will be a certain 'assymmetry' between the kind of explanation required for the achievement of the goal, on the one hand, and the failure of a functional system to do so on the other.

> Teleological explanation places one result among those which are ideally possible for a system in a special position. For that the system achieves this result-condition neither calls for nor admits of explanation; but should it achieve any other condition, we are bound to give an account...Abnormal functioning must bring in a set of laws linking interfering factors and non-normal conditions which are not teleological.[1]

> The intentional stance is not suited to accounting for breakdowns in normal functioning[2]...When a response to the environment is inappropriate it 'makes no sense', hence no intentional (putatively sense making) account will be justified.[3]

That 'non-normal' results are to be treated differently from 'normal' results -- indeed, that the <u>achievement</u> of the normal result does not require <u>functional</u> explanation at all -- follows, trivially, from the sort of information functional explanation provides. Functional explanation shows <u>how</u> a particular means event contributes to a certain end, and/or specifies <u>what</u> the end is, to which a particular means event is seen to be, or shown to be, a means. Thus, neither normal nor non-normal <u>results</u> are susceptible of functional explanation; there is, <u>ex hypothesi</u>, no further end by reference to which either could be functionally explained. Functional explanation of an event or process does not purport to explain how there came to be this goal directed process. Rather, it is because there are such processes, as

---

[1] Charles Taylor, <u>Behaviour</u>, p. 22.

[2] Dennett, "Intentional Systems", p. 89.

[3] Dennett, <u>Content and Consciousness</u>, p. 78.

a result of whatever causes, that functional explanation applies to anything and thus has any interest.

While functional explanation does not normally refer to causal background conditions of the system, it is surely plausible to think that it presupposes that there be suitable background conditions. (The usefulness of such explanation need violate no natural laws). Most all macro explanations seem to presuppose certain felicitous regularities in the underlying physico-chemical reality that are the sine qua non of the interest and applicability of such explanations. For example, if the radiation from the sun were too intense there simply wouldn't be any life on earth, and so biological and psychological functional explanations would be otiose. More particularly, the success of such explanations depends on creatures having nervous systems that function normally in a certain way and sensory apparatus which provides them with generally reliable beliefs about the environment. If these background conditions were to break down -- when, for example, a person suffers a stroke and dies -- then functional explanation no longer applies to her/him.

These causal background conditions are related to the functional explanation itself in an oblique way. In the normal case, they are not referred to as causes of the explinandum. Rather, they specify a setting in which the explinandum (or some functional equivalent) is required (or makes possible, or contributes to making possible) achievement of the goal. Frequently, the explinandum (the means) in such a context can be seen to be part of a series of events which causes the explanans (the end). The explanatory relation is thus the reverse of normal causal explanation; in causal explanations generally the explanans causes the explanandum.

This fact about the background conditions can be exploited in order to solve a problem that has long plagued interpretation of functional explanation. There seems to be an important difference between the function of a particular item and other things which it does which are not part of its function. These further results may even be beneficial to the system, but they are nonetheless 'accidental'. The distinction between function and accident is crucial if we are to be able to distinguish 'the real reason' for particular acts from other 'mere rationalizations' which are not in fact the reason for the act at all. ('Rationalization' is here used in the popular, not the philosopher's sense).

It has not, however, been clear how to articulate what this difference is; and thus it has not been clear whether this interpretation of action explanation could secure a suitable sense for 'the real reason'. There has been no clear basis on which to distinguish true from false functional explanations -- a rather serious lacuna. Wright,[1] however, has suggested that the distinction may be secured in the following way: y is (really) the function of x, and not merely an accidental something that x does, if the fact that x does y is (somehow or other) responsible

---

[1] "The function of a telephone is effecting rapid, convenient communication. But there are many other things telephones do: take up space on my desk, disturb me at night, absorb and reflect light, and so forth." Larry Wright, "Functions", The Philosophical Review, Vol. LXXXII, No. 2 (April, 1973), p. 141.

for x's being there. Thus, the contrast between functional explanations and normal causal explanations is rather different from what has often been thought. It is not a distinction between explanations having to do with etiology and explanations having (entirely) to do with something else. Rather, both involve etiological claims, but claims of different kinds. A functional explanation suggests that there is a kind of etiology for the item it explains; normal causal explanations spell that etiology out. It is a difference of more and less specific etiological commitments, between more and less immediate etiologies.

Reference to background is frequently left implicit, and even when explicit is seldom very detailed. This is partly because they are assumed to be satisfied in 'normal conditions'; adopting the functional stance "pays off when we have reason to suppose the assumption of optimal design is warranted". But lack of detail in reference to these conditions also reflects lack of relevant knowledge. We often do not know the causal chains connecting particular environmental conditions with the occurrence of the explinandum, and connecting both, in turn, with achievement of the goal. Brown characterizes intentional systems as "systems into which known or obvious causal chains disappear". And Dennett, adopting the functional stance also 'pays off' when "we doubt the practicality of prediction from the physical stance".[1] One may refer to 'something of causal relevance' without knowing just what the causal chains are.

Specific reference to background conditions, however, becomes teleologically crucial in their absence. In order to explain the <u>malfunction</u> of systems we need to locate an event which occurred, and which

---

[1] D. C. Dennett, "Intentional Systems", p. 92; Brown, <u>Action</u>.

was not part of any suitable chain of means-events to the goal. Often this is an event which interfered with, or prevented, the occurrence of any suitable such chain. "It is from the physical stance alone that we can predict and explain the malfunction of systems."[1]

The particular nature of the non-normal background condition explains the particular nature of the non-normal result. Excess radiation or very extreme temperatures, we have noted, usually result in dead plants, the cessation of all functional regularities. But the regularities may also break down without breaking down completely; a stroke may fail to kill a person and merely leave her/him partly paralyzed. In such a case we may explain the particular disability by reference to particular brain areas.

Less drastically, drugs or alcohol, by temporarily inhibiting propagation of certain nerve impulses, account for other (usually temporary) sorts of systemmic malfunctions. *Qua* non-normal for the individual or species, we explain the behaviour by reference to the causal background, and physical effects of the stroke or the drug. But *qua* a kind of (albeit idiosyncratic) functioning we may also discern functional regularities therein. Less drastically still, if a person is apparently normal, not suicidal, but reaches for a glass of toxic dye, we may explain this abnormal functioning by appeal to the agent's mistaken belief that the glass contained kool-aid. Most action theorists appeal to just this feature to explain the most modest dislocation of functional regularities, particularly when the regularities that remain seem quite regular nonetheless. Goldman suggests that in irrational

---

[1] D. C. Dennett, "Intentional Systems", p. 88.

action an agent "may forget an important consideration in bringing a complicated process of deliberation to a close", or "standing wants may not be brought to bear". And Hempel:

> Even if the agent were to take into account all aspects of his total goal as well as all the relevant information at his disposal, and even if he should go through a deliberate "calculation of means to be adopted toward his chosen end"...the result may still fail to be a rational decision because of some logical flaw in his calculations.[1]

The background assumption of optimal design in the case of intentional systems includes importantly the assumption that persons will make rational inferences and believe truths. Falsehood of one or another of these conditions can account for the very particular sort of malfunction represented by apparently irrational action.

In conclusion, our interpretation of action explanation as a form of functional explanation has the following theoretical virtues. It enjoys three virtues also claimed by the want theorist. First, our interpretation relates action explanation to explanation in other fields. It is not the case that we must choose between a straightforward causal account and a 'sui generis' one; functional explanation is another, legitimate, form of explanation which has a wide usefulness. Second, Wright has provided us with a way to locate 'the real reason' within functional explanation, and to distinguish it from mere rationalizations. It is not only straightforward causal accounts which are able to do this. Third, our action explanation does not leave it a brute but happy fact that when one performs an action one's _body_ does any one of

---

[1] Alvin Goldman, A Theory of Human Action, p. 108. Carl G. Hempel, Aspects of Scientific Explanation, p. 476.

the range of things that could be a case of that action. An explanation of the action suggests an account of the bodily movement because the action just is the movement functionally characterized.

These *desiderata* are secured without the overreaching that got the want theorist into trouble. In particular, we are not required to seek a 'common coin' for psychological antecedents of action, which common coin seems not to be available. Nor does the functional theorist construe psychological states as needing themselves to be 'forceful' or 'energetic' and thus capable of moving to action. There is energy enough in muscle contractions, derived from metabolized food. We have neither need nor use for energetic bits of non-physical, not-clockwork in addition. A cost, of course, is that the functional account is not particularly well-suited to account for reports of the experience of inner struggle and turmoil in acting. But then this has not proven to be a high ranking *desideratum*. Feelings of strife and anxiety are inessential embellishments even in the case of conflicted action, as Davidson remarks. And surely we do not want a general theory which *requires* any such lively inner show as part of the account in general. Indeed, it would be quite exhausting if our inner lives were regularly lively in anything like that kind of way!

Because functional explanation does not explain events in terms of antecedent events which cause them, our ignorance of psychological processing (if there is such) does not trouble the success of action explanation. The main illumination comes from relating the act to some suitable goal; the kind of reference made to etiology is vague enough to be safe.

Finally, this interpretation of action explanation allows us to avoid the nihilism of explanation to which Davidson's general theory succumbs. The mental is not, in fact, all _that_ anomalous; and we have located a way to set out the requisite explanatory generalizations which are both defensible and illuminating.

### C. Final causes and akrasia

We now have before us what I take to be an adequate account of the general structure of action explanation. We turn now to consider whether open-eyed akrasia is compatible with this good general theory. Let us review briefly the conditions which define open-eyed akrasia. The question is whether actions satisfying the following four conditions are compatible with the general theory of action: a) the agent does x intentionally, and for the akratic reason _simpliciter_; b) the agent believes that there is an alternative action y open to her/him; c) the agent judges that, all things considered, it would be better to do y than to do x; and d) the agent regrets having performed the action.

Intuitively, this amounts to the claim that an agent sometimes does x for a reason, but the agent judges that that reason, under the circumstances is not a very good one. The akratic reason need not be bad in itself: the act omitted need not be morally better, prudentially better, or more in accord with accepted social norms. Considerations like these may or may not matter to a particular akrates. Rather, the akratic reason need only be judged to be the _lesser_ reason. _Whatever_ the goals of a particular akrates, the akratic reason has been taken into account and outweighed by all the reasons believed relevant to the situation at hand. Given the things that matter to a particular akrates, whatever they are, the cost of acting on the akratic reason is judged by the akrates to be not worth it. The cost may or may not be moral turpitude or social ostracism; it is <u>essentially</u> only sacrifice of the more important goal to the lesser.

Given this characterization of akratic acts, it is easy to see why open-eyed akrasia presents at least a <u>prima facie</u> strain on the explanatory potential of teleological explanation. Whether or not we decide that open-eyed akrasia is in fact possible, this fact can explain the Socratic side of our intuitions. Acts are explained, according to this theory, by exhibiting their believed contribution to the goals of the person whose action is being explained. When there is conflict acts are explained by reference either to the higher ranking or the more inclusive goal. But a case of akrasia is precisely an act which the agent judges to not contribute to her/his higher ranking goal. Worse, it is not merely a gratuitous act, neither here nor there with respect to any significant aims. Quite the contrary, it is an act which is judged to conflict with and damage the goals that matter more.

It is no less easy to see the attraction of the skeptic's move to relieve this strain. A standard skeptical move is to insist that the akrates temporarily becomes unaware of the fact that the akratic act damages a higher goal. The akrates is actually aware only of the fact that there's something to be said for the akratic act. Appropriate adjustments in facts realized by the agent at the time of action are the standard first move in explaining irrational action generally. This kind of adjustment is especially to be sought when the agent is not mad, drunk, or tripping on drugs, appears in many respects to be functioning normally, and the action that is performed appears to be intentional. Indeed, the only anomaly with the akratic act, in many cases, is that that act conflicts with the purposes that characterize the person.

But those of our intuitions which suggest that open-eyed akrasia is of course possible would be done less than justice if we opted now for the skeptic's solution. We must investigate whether there is not another, less strongly counter-intuitive way of easing the theoretical strain. We shall consider three of the best so far proposed, in increasing order of complexity and sophistication.

Anscombe remarks, in "Thought and Action in Aristotle", that people's ends are not nearly so clear-cut and well-defined as we, (and the skeptic), have so far represented them as being. The skeptic's perception of the need for radical remedies, to account for akrasia, is mistaken. It arises from an unduly rigid view of the kind of functional system that a person is. She develops this criticism in <u>Intention</u>:

> Ancient and medieval philosophers -- or some of them at any rate — regarded it as evident, demonstrable, that human beings must always act with some end in view, and even with some one end in view. The argument for this strikes us as rather strange. Can't a man just do what he does, a great deal of the time? He may or may not have a reason or a purpose; and if he has a reason or a purpose, it in turn may just be what he happens to want; why demand a reason or purpose <u>for it</u>? And why must

>we arrive at some <u>one</u> purpose that has an intrinsic finality about it? The old arguments were designed to show that the chain could not go on forever; they pass us by, because we are not inclined to think it <u>must</u> even begin; and it can surely stop where it stops, no need for it to stop at a purpose that looks intrinsically final, one and the same for all actions.[1]

A person, and her/his actions, are not to be construed as one large, all-encompassing, functional system, according to Anscombe. It is foolish to suppose that all actions may be explained by reference to a single goal. Rather, persons quite obviously have, and act for, many different ends. The relations between these ends are frequently vague and indeterminate. There is thus nothing special about akrasia; it is but one of many instances of acting for an end which is not 'ultimate'.

Whatever the merits of Anscombe's general view, surely akrasia is not even a member of the class of acts she indicates here. A case of akrasia involves only the conflict of what the agent believes to be a lesser with a greater good. Hence, any indeterminacy in general in people's ends is quite irrelevant. Indeed, the very possibility of such a judgment, which is part of the definition of akrasia, <u>requires</u> that there be stronger relations between ends than Anscombe seems willing to allow. There must be a priority ranking between <u>some</u> ends if one is to be able to do the worse.

There probably are persons whose ends are indeterminate in the way that Anscombe suggests. They simply have not ordered, or have chosen to not order, their goals in any hierarchical pattern. Such

---

[1] G. E. M. Anscombe, "Thought and Action in Aristotle", in <u>New Essays on Plato and Aristotle</u>, ed. Renford Bambrough (London: Routledge and Kegan Paul, 1975); Anscombe, <u>Intention</u>, pp. 33-34.

persons, however, are never akratic with respect to these unordered ends. In this respect, they are like the virtuous person, although for different reasons. Such persons would simply not judge one act to be better than another. Consequently, it is not their behaviour that we are investigating. Anscombe has not provided an alternative account of akrasia; it is not an account of akrasia at all.

A second attempt to resolve the <u>prima facie</u> difficulty about open-eyed akrasia is more to the point. John Cooper and Gilbert Harman present views which both avoid Anscombe's mistake, and purport to render open-eyed akrasia compatible with our general beliefs about action as set out above.[1] Both restrict themselves to cases where the agent does make a comparative value judgment, and thus to actions that are judged by the agent to be worse than some available alternative. They attempt to show how such acts can be accommodated within the general explanatory framework. Both argue that the apparent difficulty arises because we have assumed that only reasons that show an act to be better 'all things considered' can adequately explain an action. This assumption, they think, is mistaken. This is one, but only one, way of securing a suitable goal; there are others.

John Cooper suggests that an act of open-eyed akrasia is explained simply by citing the <u>prima facie</u> reason that it's pleasant (or socially graceful etc. ... whatever the akratic reason happens to be), so far as reasons explain it at all. He simply thinks it's unnecessary to insist, as the skeptic does insist, that the person has <u>also</u> temporarily

---

[1] John Cooper, lectures at Harvard University, spring 1973; Gilbert Harman, "Davidson on How Weakness of Will is Possible", unpublished paper.

lost sight of reasons on the whole. The seeming contradiction between a functional account of action, and the existence of open-eyed akrasia is only apparent. Intentional action and its explanation require only that a person act for some goal. This the akrates clearly does. 'Minimal rationality' is satisfied if there is some reason a person can give for her/his intentional action. It does not require overwhelmingly good reason. Indeed, it is compatible with a person's being fully aware that she/he has overwhelmingly good reason to refrain from the action.

This proposal, of course, raises an utterly fundamental issue about the nature of functional explanation of action. In particular, it forces us to confront in more detail the question of how functional explanation should be adapted to account for the complex activities of intentional systems. Persons *qua* practical agents, we have noted, unlike persons *qua* biological organisms (and especially unlike functional systems that are artifacts) clearly have a multiplicity of ends, and these ends may on occasion conflict. How does functional explanation apply to cases where more than one goal is at issue, and their requirements are in conflict?

One way to approach this matter is to ask what kinds of psychological ascriptions are required for suitable goals. Does the fact that something is merely wanted provide an explanatory goal? Or must it be more wanted? Or most wanted? Or judged attractive, or better, or best? It is surely possible that the goal specified by the lesser reason may yet be what the agent wants more, or most, at least at the moment, or judges attractive, though it is probably not possible that that goal be judged better or best. Thus, the specification of the right kind of goal will prove crucial to the success of Cooper's account of akrasia.

Endless disputes have raged about the relative priority of wants and practical judgments in action explanation. At the two extremes are Hume, who insisted that reason alone was 'inert', 'indolent' and quite incapable of motivating, and Socrates, who focused instead on an appeal to the good (or at least the apparent good). In fact I do not think it matters whether one refers to the goal required for action explanation in terms of wants or practical beliefs so long as one does not draw any wrong inferences. Keeping both notions to the fore can help in this respect; that's part of the reason the pair of principles P1, (mentioning wants) and P2, (mentioning practical judgments), is attractive.

The crucial point is that certain systematic connections be preserved -- connections between psychological states themselves and between these states and actions. Both practical judgments and explanatory wants are attributed in such a way that we are best able to account for the behaviour of an agent. Neither may plausibly be attributed willy-nilly out of such connection to patterns of behaviour. The assumption of rationality is a structural feature of the explanatory framework. Thus, it would seem that when goals are believed to be in conflict, when comparative judgments or desires are at issue, then the goal needed in explanation will be what's wanted more or thought better, and not merely wanted or thought attractive.

But, Cooper might reply, surely these descriptions may pull apart. Any is this not precisely the plight of the akrates: sometimes she/he wants more to do what she/he judges to be the worse. In such a case, according to this proposal, what is <u>only wanted</u> more (and not also thought better) suffices to fix a suitable goal for the explanation.

But it is the <u>interpretation</u> of this plight that is precisely the point at issue between the skeptic and the believer in open-eyed akrasia. If Cooper were to insist that open-eyed akrasia is possible and that here (if not elsewhere) reference to greater desire <u>simpliciter</u> explains it, he would simply beg the question against the skeptic. And this scheme <u>in general</u> of course does not work. One quite reasonably balks at so thin a notion of evaluation in general. A crucial part of our reason for attributing beliefs about what's better, we have argued, is the action of the person. It is not for nothing that we refuse to make such ascriptions on the basis of words alone. Secondly, instances abound where we simply do not want to do, and cannot make ourselves want to do what we think it better to do. But we do what we think better nonetheless. Such is the stuff of continence. Such instances are no less damaging for this version of functional explanation than they were for Goldman's want theory. In the face of such counterexamples, Neil Cooper expands the notion of a 'want'.

> The word 'want' is used here in a minimal sense, in which it can be applied to anything one is in favor of for any reason whatsoever, as opposed to the Kantian sense, in which it is applied to anything one has a natural urge or inclination towards.[1]

---

[1] Neil Cooper, "Oughts and Wants" in <u>Weakness of Will</u>, ed. G. W. Mortimore (London, 1971), p. 195.

But the penalty of this move here is no less costly than it was for our previous want theorists. The price of avoiding ready falsification is vacuity. In this sense of 'want' a person surely does intentionally all and only those acts she/he most 'minimally' wants to do. But this is only because what she/he most 'minimally' wants to do in a situation is whatever it is she/he in fact intentionally does.

Any theorist who insists that what one most wants can and often does diverge from what one thinks best, and that this can account for open-eyed akrasia, is probably appealing to <u>something other than</u> an explanatory use of either notion. An explanatory use of both is governed importantly by larger patterns of behaviour; both notions are to be distinguished from related, but not identical, notions whose attribution is not similarly restricted. Practical judgments are not mere 'entertainments of ideas'; nor are explanatory wants either phenomenologically 'maximal' wants or Cooper's 'minimal' wants. Given the temptations to slide in any of these directions in explaining action one can appreciate Aristotle's introduction of the technical terms 'choice', which he defined as either desiring reason or ratiocinative desire indifferently. It is the need for <u>both</u> notions in explanation that P1 and P2 also emphasize. For our purposes, however, it seems that referring to a suitable goal as something 'thought better' is less misleading (when explicated as we have done in Chapter I) than referring to it as something 'wanted more' -- but this is only because the temptations to these wrong inferences are less strong.

What is left of Cooper's account of open-eyed akrasia if functional explanation is not encumbered with this bloated notion of a want and anemic interpretation of practical judgment? It would seem to amount to the claim that a practical judgment that x is to be done <u>some</u> things considered can explain an act, as well as a practical judgment <u>all</u> things considered. In a case of conflict between ends, either the higher ranking or the lower may be cited in explanation. Interpreted in this way, however, the proposal takes us directly back to theory sketch A (Chapter III, pp. 95-96) with all of its bizarre consequences. It is a Herculean labor to describe an action that has <u>nothing</u> to recommend it. St. Francis might torture small birds; he has <u>a</u> reason in that he might learn something of aid to others who are wounded. One might nibble Belladonna, or leap from a flying aircraft; surely the knowledge to be gained, of what it is like, provides <u>a</u> reason for doing both. Cooper's proposal, like A, fails to pick out any one act, or any delimited group of acts, as opposed to indefinitely many others. It allows us to 'explain' indefinitely many acts which patently cannot be explained in this fashion. This proposal, like A, is surely a non-controversial paradigm case of a vacuous theory. There is no even describable action, the performance of which would falsify it.

Harman provides a modification of this proposal which delimits the class of acceptable explanations somewhat. He does not accept just any reason as explanatory of just any action. Rather, he suggests, akrasia is to be explained by citing the akratic reason together with an account of what the akrates <u>does with</u> the lesser reason.

> In a sense the incontinent man counts a consideration twice. That's why we call him irrational. He counts it once in deciding what is better, all things considered, but then he counts it again in arriving at what he wants all things considered. This explains why we are inclined to think that the incontinent man attaches too much weight to one of his desires -- not that he attaches too much weight to the desire when he decides what it is better to do; but rather that <u>in a sense he considers it twice in arriving at his overall desire</u>. For his overall desire is based on two considerations: eg. 1) that all things considered (including his irrational nagging desire to brush his teeth) it would be better to stay in bed, and 2) that he has an irrational nagging desire to brush his teeth.[1]

Thus, it is only those lesser reasons upon which a certain operation is performed, viz. counting twice, that can be explanatory.

Harman's proposal derives part of its intuitive plausibility from the introduction of a "desire, all things considered". However, as we have seen, this is a move of which we should be wary. A desire 'based on considerations' looks like Aristotle's 'rational desire', or 'choice', but Harman introduces it without any of the necessary constraints. In fact, it <u>functions</u> just like Neil Cooper's 'minimal want'. The facility of its introduction vitiates any explanatory power. This basic fault can be highlighted by considering its consequences.

We are given no reason to doubt that this operation, 'counting twice', might be performed on any reason whatsoever. Thus, it still seems likely that quite literally <u>no</u> action is ruled out. Cruelty from St. Francis can be explained as well as kindness; suicidal behaviour on the part of those not suicidal. Each of these reasons, it would seem, may as well be counted twice as garden variety akratic reasons.

---

[1] Gilbert Harman, "Davidson on How Weakness of Will is Possible", unpublished paper, pp. 11-12.

Surely the device of counting twice cannot restore explanatory adequacy to any of these patently non-explanatory 'explanations'. The real trouble with this proposal lies at its source. As Davidson has noted, we do not want to explain akrasia as a logical error. We cannot divorce a reason, any old reason, from its context of the particular aims and purposes characteristic of the person whose act is being explained. The content of reasons, and their relation to the content of these aims and purposes, cannot be ignored. This should be obvious, since the illumination provided by reason explanation precisely consists in relating a particular act, properly described, to such aims and purposes.

But still, is it not unduly restrictive to insist that only good reasons can explain actions? The counter-examples that tell against Harman are bizarre, outré, in a way that akratic acts are not. Can we not locate some way of connecting lesser -- but in themselves perfectly comprehensible -- reasons to the psychological system in general? Can we not suggest some way of explaining something less than pristinely rational acts? It may be fair to insist that the explanation requires more than merely the lesser reason alone. But can we not supplement this with an appeal to natural facts, other than an operation of 'counting twice', and which are not themselves reasons? Can we not appeal to natural facts connected to the content of akratic reasons themselves to explain why the lesser reason was nonetheless the goal pursued?

A theoretically significant distinction between akrasia and the bizarre counter-examples is not yet made out. To be sure, the akratic reason would explain the akratic act did the agent not also see better reason to refrain. But then 'to find out what it's like' would also explain leaping from a flying airplane, or tasting Belladonna, too, were it not that the agent also saw better reason to refrain. What natural facts might suggest an explanation of open-eyed akrasia? Gerasimos Santas has attempted to develop an account along these lines.

He is not so rash as to suggest that any old reason, abstracted from its content, and divorced from its context, will do, even counted twice, thrice, or a hundred times. He does suggest, however, that an appeal to reasons 'all things considered' is unduly restricted. Empirical psychology has shown, he says, that "knowledge or belief of the relative values of the objects" is only one of several factors relevant to the explanation of a particular act. Any theory which omits these further factors, as Aristotle seems to, is an "oversimplification'.

> ...Other factors are the firmness of the knowledge or beliefs, the estimated probabilities that the values will obtain, the distance in space and/or time of the subject from the valued objects, and sometimes the initial physiological condition of the subject.[1]

Thus, we can explain a case of acting on a lesser reason if any member of this clearly delimited set of further conditions obtains.

In order to evaluate Santas' proposal, we must first note some distinctions that he does not. The judgment "x is better to do than y,

---

[1] Gerasimos Santas, "Aristotle on Practical Inference, the Explanation of Action and Akrasia", Phronesis, Vol. XIV, No. 2 (1969), pp. 188-189.

all things considered" is not equivalent to "x aims at A, and I think (hope, fear, pray), but am not sure, that A is more valuable than anything else I can aim at just now". Nor is the former judgment equivalent to a more confident version of the latter: "x aims at A, and A is more valuable than anything else I can aim at just now".

An original Rembrandt is more valuable than a book of Rembrandt reproductions. I have ten dollars to spend. With it I may either buy a book of Rembrandt reproductions, or I may buy two tickets to a raffle of an original Rembrandt. Two actions are open to me; one aims at something clearly more valuable than the other. It surely does not follow that, all things considered, it is better for me to buy two tickets to the raffle than to buy the book of reproductions. Judgments between people would vary enormously on which act is better, despite unanimity on which object is more valuable. The divergence between the value of the object and the wisdom of the choice takes a different form if I think that the painting to be raffled may well be a fake.

Santas might complain that he has been misunderstood. The 'objects' that he means are not the painting and the book of reproductions. Rather, the appropriate objects are "having a one in a million chance of acquiring a Rembrandt", or a fake Rembrandt, on the one hand, and "acquiring the book of reproductions" on the other. It is the value, to the agent, of the <u>state of affairs</u> produced by the act, and not any simple material object, to which we must attend.

If this is Santas view, then he has not provided us with the list of independent factors that he promised. "Firmness of the knowledge of belief", and "estimated probabilities that the values will obtain" are not factors <u>other than</u> any belief about the relative values of the objects, if 'objects' are construed in this second way. Indeed, they are important constituents of that belief. Surely considerations such as these are ones that any reasonable person would take into account in deciding on the best course of action. Akrasia consists in acting against a judgment which has <u>already incorporated</u> vicissitues such as these.

What of the third factor -- "distance in space and time of the subject from the valued object"? A part of its importance, of course, is connected to the estimated probability that the value will obtain. One is prudent to make weaker predictions regarding next year than regarding next week. But surely there is more to it than that. I can predict with a high degree of certainty that chocolate eclairs now will result in fat next month; that heavy smoking now will result in physiological damage next year. There does seem to be something in the claim that persons sometimes discount future bad consequences even when precarious probabilities are not involved. But what is there in the claim?

It is clearly not a matter of mere futurity. This can be shown easily by reviewing the awkward counter-examples that plagued the Cooper/Harman view. There is <u>a</u> reason, it seems, though not a very good one, for tasting Belladonna or for leaping from an airplane. One could acquire knowledge of what Belladonna tastes like, and of what falling feels like. This knowledge is something that would be gained immediately; the death, by contrast, is somewhere in the future. Further discussion of this 'further factor' may well await a more detailed exposition of precisely what the factor is.

It is difficult to evaluate Santas' final condition -- "the initial physiological condition of the subject" -- because of its vagueness. Clearly the physiological condition cannot be such as to preclude the possibility of (strongly) intentional action altogether -- a condition such as tripping on drugs, drunkenness, or an epileptic seizure. This is because the subject must be capable of performing a strongly intentional akratic act. One would need to know in more detail exactly what physiological facts Santas means, and how they operate.

Thus, I think that Santas' proposed account of akrasia is no more successful than any of the foregoing. Two of his 'further factors' have turned out to be simply irrelevant; the remaining two too vague to evaluate properly. Further consideration of this kind of proposal may fairly await a more precise articulation of what the proposal amounts to.

A more limited claim that 'physiological facts', or some other kind of biological explanation explain the akrates' intentionally acting on the lesser reason may be a promising line to pursue. However, it is not obviously an alternative to a Socratic account of akrasia. It is not clear that such an account would be non-Socratic rather than Socratic. One would think it obvious that such an account would be non-Socratic only if one is <u>already</u> committed to the falsity of Socrates.

***

We have, to this point, considered all of the strongest extant attempts to provide an account of open-eyed akrasia. The course of our inquiry is littered with their failures. At this point, I think it is fair to argue that the burden of proof has been strongly shifted from those who, like Socrates and Aristotle, deny the possibility of open-eyed akrasia, to those who insist that it does, of course, exist.

We noted in Chapter I that our pre-theoretic intuitions as to whether open-eyed akrasia exists are in fact strongly ambivalent. We argued that a necessary condition of resolving this ambivalence, and articulating the real nature of akrasia, is to produce a respectable account of the phenomena under the favored description (i.e. open-eyed or as the skeptic describes it). It seems that there is no good account of open-eyed akrasia available at present; those that have been proposed conflict with the best account of action explanation. It is only reasonable now to consider the details of the most plausible skeptic's case: to consider the description offered, and the theoretical underpinnings of that account. Aristotle will prove the most fruitful skeptic to consider.

I shall argue that Aristotle's account of the Socratic phenomenon is very much more powerful than has yet been appreciated; it is much less counter-intuitive than has generally been thought. These virtues, I shall argue, should be sufficient to persuade us that akrasia may well exist only in the Socratic variety; they may even be sufficient to persuade us that it does.

It is possible, of course, that a new and better account of open-eyed akrasia will be developed in the future. When such an account is available, the debate should begin again. A clear statement of the strengths of the skeptics case should raise the level of that debate; this is an improvement which is sorely needed. If open-eyed akrasia can in fact be accounted for, and thus countenanced, this account should include an account of why part of our intuitions are so strongly inclined to deny it.

My strategy for defending the skeptics case is the following: I shall review briefly the theoretically significant elements in Aristotle's account of akrasia.[1] Then I shall exhibit the theoretical elegance of these elements within his general theory of action. Aristotle's general theory is of a piece with the one that we have concluded is the most powerful on independent grounds. In view of the theoretical elegance of this fit, and the failure of proposed alternatives to fit at all, I suggest that it is highly plausible to conclude that the best general theory of action requires an Aristotelian account of akrasia. This hypothesis is then strengthened by showing how his account of akrasia fits nicely with the wide range of our intuitions which are Socratic. Finally, I shall consider the most pressing of the objections that have been raised against Aristotle's account, and show how they can be met.

---

[1] It is all too common in Aristotelian scholarship that the precise details of any particular interpretation are likely to be controversial. His account of akrasia is no exception. There are those who insist that Aristotle is not a skeptic at all, but rather provides some account of open-eyed akrasia. I cannot, in the time available, address all the points in the text where this interpretation and mine would diverge; textual scholarship is also not our primary purpose. Instead, I shall indicate only a few of the more salient disputed points.

Brevity here will not be seriously prejudicial. There are, to be sure, some remarks which lend themselves more naturally to a non-Socratic interpretation, such as those in I. 13 and III. 2. There are parts of the discussion in Book VII which could go either way. But a non-Socratic interpretation of Aristotle is not usually motivated in the first instance by being the most natural reading of the text. Quite the contrary. It is more often motivated instead by the principle of charity in historical scholarship, together with the belief that a Socratic account is incorrect. Thus, interpretive efforts are directed to showing that Aristotle did not in fact propose that sort of account. Our results suggest that such charity is misdirected. It is not obvious that we do Aristotle a favor by reading a non-Socratic account into the <u>Ethics</u>. Indeed, I think that we do him a disservice.

CHAPTER V

THE ARISTOTELIAN AKRATES

Book VII, 1-10 of the Nicomachean Ethics contains Aristotle's most detailed and extended discussion of akrasia. There are scattered references elsewhere in the Ethics, in the De Anima, the Politics and the Rhetoric. But none of these contexts compare with the detail or theoretical sophisticiation of the Book VII account. Thus, in setting out Aristotle's view this is the obvious place to begin.

The discussion of akrasia is one of the most thorough instances of Aristotle's general philosophical method of dialectic. Roughly, the method consists in setting out the 'phainomena' (things commonly said and believed about akrasia, including the views of other theorists); noting and discussing difficulties that arise for any of them, or contradictions that obtain between them; and formulating his own account out of a resolution of these difficulties. Some of the phainomena are characteristically rejected; some of the difficulties shown to be only apparent.

> We must, as in all other cases, set the appearances before us, and, after first discussing the difficulties, go on to prove, if possible, the truth of all the common opinions about these affections of the mind, or, failing this, of the greater number and the most authoritative; for if we both refute the objections and leave the common opinions undisturbed, we shall have proved the case sufficiently. (1145b1-7)

## A. Analysis of EN VII

### 1. Preparatory moves

First, Aristotle introduces the things that are said about akrasia by common persons in ordinary contexts. "The incontinent man, knowing that what he does is bad, does it as a result of passion, while the continent man, knowing that his appetites are bad, refuses on account of his rational principle to follow them" (1145b12-15). The akrates is ready to "abandon the result of his calculations" (1145b11). These are views on the nature of akrasia that accord well with remarks elsewhere in the Ethics: "The impulses of incontinent people move them in contrary directions" (1102b23)..."they choose, instead of things they themselves think good, things that are pleasant but hurtful" (1166b8). In the De Anima Aristotle says, "One appetency prevails over another appetency in the case where incontinence has supervened" (DA434a12-15). Yet, the akrates is not to be viewed as one who is literally overcome, for "the akrates acts rather voluntarily and not from force" (EE1224a38).

The experience of Greek citizens, it seems is similar to that appealed to by Sidgwick, Davidson, and the rest (Chapter I, p. 7). That is, it seems to include cases of intentional (Aristotle would say 'voluntary') action which is recognized to be contrary to one's own practical principles, one's considered judgments of what it would be better to do. Some of the above passages suggest an 'active struggle' between contrary impulses in which practical reason is sometimes the loser; others simply describe the result, the performance of an action which the actor knows is bad.

The common opinions, asserting the existence of 'action contrary to knowledge' in a fairly straightforward sense, are then confronted with Socrates' denial that there is any such phenomenon, or, at least, one answering to the description that has so far been proposed. "Socrates was entirely opposed to the view in question, holding that there is no such thing as incontinence" (1145b25). Socrates had claimed, though himself well aware of the common opinions, that:

> Knowledge is such as to rule a man, and nobody who knows that is good and bad can be so mastered by anything as to act contrary to what knowledge commands. (That which the many describe as) enslavement to oneself is nothing but ignorance and mastery of oneself is nothing but wisdom...and we define ignorance as having a false belief and being mistaken. (<u>Protagoras</u> 352c3-7; 358c1-6)

The dialectical method itself would allow Aristotle to reject either Socrates' view, or the common opinions, or to reinterpret each in a fashion that would enable him to reconcile them. He indicates at once that he is partial to Socrates. He says first that Socrates "plainly contradicts the <u>phainomena</u>", but then proceeds to 'inquire... what is the manner of [the akrates'] ignorance" (1145b28-30). And again in Chapter 3: "We must consider first, then, whether incontinent people act knowingly or not, and in what sense knowingly" (1146b8). The entire discussion is devoted to "in what sense knowingly", it being assumed that there is something unusual.

Given Aristotle's lack of a Socratic taste for paradox, and his characteristic down-to-earth common sense, this strong partiality to Socrates may legitimately appear puzzling. And he does not here, nor anywhere else in the <u>Ethics</u>, explain why he favors that view. (The explanation, if there is one, must be constructed from other sources).

Aristotle's only criticism is that the view requires a minor qualification. The akrates does not have any <u>ordinary</u> kind of false, or mistaken, belief about how to act; there is at least that much to the common opinion that the akrates does know better. "That the man who behaves incontinently does not, before he gets into this state, think he ought so to act, is evident" (1145b30). This however is not actually a disagreement with Socrates at all. He surely would agree with Aristotle that the akrates does not <u>in general</u> think he ought to act in the way in which he does when acting akratically. The akrates is surely to be distinguished from the profligate person. The mistaken belief of the akrates is, at best, a temporary one, as Aristotle seems to be suggesting here.

He next sets aside two facile ways in which the common opinions and Socrates' views may be reconciled. Some are prepared to grant, he says, Socrates' claim that no one can act against <u>knowledge</u>, but think that his insistence on ignorance is unnecessary regarding the less exalted cognitive state of <u>opinion</u>. (It is arguable that opinion, and not knowledge, is all that the <u>hoi polloi</u> discussed in the <u>Protagoras</u> can lay claim to; hence Socrates need not have insisted that their opinions temporarily reverse themselves when acting akratically). Aristotle replies that this distinction between knowledge and opinion is quite irrelevant to the point at issue. A term like the 'judgment' of our Chapter I -- lacking this ambiguity -- would seem to better suit his purposes.

If one means by 'opinion' a view on which the agent is unsettled or hesitant (and thus not a judgment) "we sympathize with (a person's) failure to stand by such a conviction...but we do not sympathize with any of the blameworthy states" (1146a1-5). Akrasia is a blameworthy state. If, on the other hand, one means by 'opinion' a practical belief which is either not true, or not well-founded, and thereby not knowledge (but nonetheless a judgment), it should be no more easily acted against than knowledge: "for some people when in a state of opinion do not hesitate, but think they know exactly...as is shown by the case of Hericlitus".(1146b25-3) Thus, if one finds the view implausible regarding firmly held opinion, one has no reason to grant it regarding knowledge. And, if one is prepared to grant it regarding knowledge, one ought also to grant it regarding opinion, construed in the only relevant sense.

Aristotle remarks that everyone is prepared to agree with Socrates that practical widsom cannot be acted against akratically:

> Is it then practical wisdom whose resistance is mastered? That is the strongest of all states. But this is absurd; the same man will be at once practically wise and incontinent, but no one would say it is part of the practically wise man to do willingly the basest acts. (1143a4-9)

But the dispute is not to be trivialized, and thus resolved, by splitting this hair of varieties of practical intellect either. Socrates is not just asserting, non-controversially, that phronesis cannot be acted against. The phroni-mos is never akratic; "...it has been shown before that the man of practical wisdom is one who will act". But Socrates is offering an account of akrasia. Phronesis cannot be acted against; but it cannot be 'temporarily lost' either. Both Socrates and the common opinions must be taken as referring to some <u>other</u> condition of practical intellect than <u>phronesis</u>; about this state there is real disagreement.[1]

## 2. Aristotle's account

Aristotle thus takes it that the dialectial problem has been set. The only difficulty explicitly located with the common opinions is that Socrates had asserted, and argued for, the contradictory claim. Two easy attempts at resolving the disagreement have been briefly shown to be inadequate. Aristotle then proceeds, in Chapter 3, to what is generally agreed to be the core of his own account of "how a man who judges rightly can act incontinently". I shall argue that EN VII, 3 is most plausibly construed as arguing for a modified Socratic account of akrasia.[2] I take Aristotle to claim that there is a (or several) natural sense(s) in which a person may both have knowledge, as the common folk had maintained, and also not have it, as Socrates had insisted. Thus,

---

[1] It is not clear just <u>what</u> this condition of practical intellect is. It does not fit neatly into the taxonomy Aristotle elsewhere sets out.

[2] As was mentioned above, this interpretation is controversial. There are those who interpret this passage in an anti-Socratic fashion. As usual with Aristotle, the disagreement is not surprising; the text is woefully incomplete at several crucial points. A part of the dispute turns on the relation between four clearly discernable sections to the argument: 1146b30-34, 1146b35-1147a9, 1147a10-24, and 1147a25-b19. In the first three passages Aristotle discusses various ways in which knowledge may be both 'had' in one sense and yet 'not had' in another sense. This would seem to be preparatory work for a modified Socratic account. However Aristotle does not say explicitly what the relation of these passages is to the fourth, and presumably crucial, one. If these three points about knowledge are exploited in the final passage, the account is Socratic. There are those, however, who urge that the first three points are not incorporated into the fourth, but are superceeded by it;

it seems that both the common folk and Socrates may be right, if akrasia always involves 'having and not having knowledge' in the sense(s) outlined.

If this description of akrasia is correct, it seems to suggest straightaway an explanation of the phenomena -- an explanation we have been seeking. The having of practical knowledge in this Pickwickian sense only (and not in the normal fashion) explains why the akrates does not do what she/he knows, in some sense of 'know', she/he should do. If ones practical knowledge is in some sense not applied to the context of action, the failure to recognize its relevance can explain the <u>failure</u> to act according to it. A further explanation is required of why the akrates does what she/he should not do. The akrates acts "in a sense willingly (1152a15)." When she/he acts akratically it is nonetheless for <u>a</u> reason. The act is done "with knowledge of what he does and the end to which he does it" (1152a15). Akrasia is a species of voluntary action. Hence there must be some other knowledge, which is not had in a Pickwickian sense only, and which explains the act that is performed. This Aristotle provides in the fourth passage.

To recap briefly our purposes here: Aristotle provides no argument here or elsewhere that this situation of 'having and not having' knowledge <u>must</u> obtain in every case of akrasia. Nonetheless, he certainly seems to believe that, and such general ignorance would be required for

---

viscissitudes of practical knowledge do not carry the <u>explanatory weight</u> in Aristotle's final account. My own view is that the best arguments support the Socratic interpretation, although these arguments fail to be conclusive.

the explanation of akrasia to work. The knowledge which is 'fully possessed' explains the akratic act <u>only</u> on condition that the 'knowledge of what is better' is <u>not</u> 'fully possessed'. In the next section we shall consider the grounds for accepting such an account; here we shall simply attend to clarifying what the account is.

a. Knowing and not knowing

In VII, 3 Aristotle moves dialectically through three kinds of complexity in the attribution of practical knowledge to a person. First, he shows that the question whether a person can 'have knowledge' of what is best, and yet act against it, is ambiguous; hence it cannot be answered with a straight 'yes' or 'no'. The opinions of both Socrates and the common people are presented too simply; the distinction is important.

> ...we use the word 'know' in two senses (for both the man who has knowledge but is not using it and he who is using it are said to know), it will make a difference whether, when a man does what he should not, he has the knowledge but is not exercising it, or <u>is</u> exercising it; for the latter seems strange but not the former. (1146b30-35)

This distinction between having and using is common in Aristotle. It is the distinction between having learned and applying a lesson, and corresponds to one of the ways in which Aristotle uses the distinction between 'actual' and 'potential' knowledge. For example, when a person has learned geometry that person has that knowledge (potentially) even when not actively engaged in solving a geometric problem. No further education is required in order to enable the student to apply it. But using in the sense of actually 'acting upon' would seem too specialized to be illuminating here. It would be tautologous to say that the akrates is not using (in this sense) knowledge she/he is currently acting against; it is unlikely that any believer would be concerned to deny that. Rather, with Walsh,[1] it seems more promising to interpret 'using' here as a kind of 'contemplating', a kind of present recognition of the bearing of ones practical knowledge on the current situation.

It is surely obvious that one knows all sorts of things that one does not 'actively contemplate' at a given time. The contents of ones consciousness at any time represent the minutest fraction of the various cognitive capacities one possesses. And there are various explanations for the fact that one does not actively contemplate particular facts. Most commonly, the practical context is simply inappropriate for their exercise. The geometer 'has' but does not contemplate her/his geometrical knowledge while engaged in polite dinner conversation. One may also fail to 'contemplate' ones practical knowledge even though it would be appropriate to the context: one may be distracted, anxious, or simply not alert; one may thereby fail to realize that that knowledge would be appropriately exercised here. One has learned to recognize such contexts; one is able (in general) to do so; one is 'potentially' able to do so here (e.g. if one were reminded). But, for various reasons that potentiality is on occasion not actualized.

Now, what would be 'strange' about acting against knowledge that one is contemplating? It clearly would be bizarre for the geometer to

---

[1] James J. Walsh, Aristotle's Conception of Moral Weakness (New York: Columbia University Press, 1963), p. 100.

contemplate the right answer and write down the wrong one, but <u>what</u> is strange about open-eyed akrasia? This question, however, amounts to a request for a justification of a Socratic account of akrasia. This Aristotle does not provide here, where he is merely setting out that account. We shall ourselves consider its justification in the next section. A part of the reason he finds it strange, though, may well be connected to the constraints noted above (Chapter 4, pp. 171.) on the ascription of **evaluative** judgments.

Aristotle's next move introduces a refinement in the kinds of knowledge which may be 'had but not used', had but not recognized or (practically) thought of in a practical context. This refinement involves "two kinds of premises" and therewith the practical syllogism.

> ...since there are two kinds of premises, there is nothing to prevent a man's having both premises and acting against his knowledge, provided that he is using only the universal premise and not the particular, for it is particular acts that have to be done. (1147a1-3)

The status of the practical syllogism in Aristotle's theory of action, and in that breakdown of rational action which we are considering, is a complicated and disputed matter to which we shall return. Since it figures importantly in the account of akrasia it merits closer attention. Aristotle here introduces a 'universal premise', containing general information such as "dry food is good for every man" or "such and such food is dry". The 'particular premise' is "this food is such and such". To know, apparently, that "such and such food is dry (and good for every person)", while in the process of eating something wet and gooey, is not "anything strange". To know, however, that "this food has properties incompatible with being dry would be extraordinary".

Certainly this refinement of things known 'only potentially' can illuminate some cases of akrasia. One may 'actually' know, for example, that too many sweets are harmful to health (a major premise) but know 'only potentially' that the eating now of this very bon-bon before me would amount to an excessive number of sweets. For other cases, however, a certain bizarre quality cannot be denied. It seems extraordinary, for example, that a person currently thinking practically about matters of diet( i.e. having 'actually' the major premise) could fail to recognize that this bit of food in his sticky fingers is certainly not dry. For someone preoccupied with other matters, and grabbing a bite on the run, the oversight might appear more plausible. But then both the universal and the particular premises would be known only potentially. The refinement would appear otiose.

But there is no need to insist that all these moves apply to all cases of akrasia. It is quite possible that this particular distinction should be invoked in some cases and not others. The introduction of the syllogism here serves at least this general function: it reminds us of the complexity of the functions of practical intellect. Practical intellect involves not only general views on the sorts of things to be pursued or avoided, but also the ability to connect these general views to concrete, particular situations. There are thus several points at which practical reason may misfunction; it need not be the same misfunction in all cases.[1]

The third step in Aristotle's development illustrates the condition of having and not using knowledge with a variety of examples (1147a8-9). He says, "It is plain, then, that incontinent people must be said to be in a similar condition to men mad, asleep, or drunk." (1147a17). All undergo some "alteration in the bodily condition" which affects their capacity to apply the practical lessons they have learned to the cases at hand. The person asleep, of course is incapable of being 'actively aware' of anything. The mad person and the drunk, by contrast, require more refined epistemelogical categories. While each may surely enjoy a conscious life, it seems unlikely that practical recognition ought to be included in that passing show. (For the sleeper and the madman the distinction between major and minor premise seems unimportant. But for the drunk her/his perception of particular facts seems more vulnerable to distortion than general practical beliefs).

One important further claim is made by use of these examples. "The use of language that flows from knowledge" by persons in such states "proves nothing" about there not being a real sense in which they are <u>not</u> actively contemplating their knowledge (1147a18). Similarly, the insistence of some akrateis that of course they do know full well that their act is the worse <u>need not</u> show straightaway that they do. Aristotle does not here appeal to any complex and overbearing theory to make room

---

[1] John Austin, "A Plea for Excuses", <u>Proceedings of Aristotelian Society</u>, Vol. LVII (1956/7), pp. 4-5, 19-20, 27.

for a Socratic account. He simply points to several other familiar contexts where we often do discount similar claims to know.

A new analogy is needed to suggest the right sort of explanation for discounting the verbal behaviour of the akrates. If the protests of the akrates "mean no more than its utterance by actors on the state" (1147a24), or a drunk reciting the verses of Empedocles,[1] then it would be tempting to think that the akrates does not <u>mean</u> her/his protestations, that she/he is perhaps hypocritical and is not in fact acting against her/his practical <u>beliefs</u>. Lines in a play, or poetry recited from memory, is not characteristically a practical <u>use</u> of language, but rather what Aristotle would call 'theorizing about practical matters'. (c.f. DA432b26-433a1; EN1142b34-1143a18). Akrasia however is defined as acting contrary to ones practical beliefs. For this purpose the example of the apprentice at a science comes closer to what Aristotle needs.

When the words of the apprentice are discounted, as not evidence for genuine practical knowledge, there is no suggestion that the person does not mean what she/he says. Rather the words are not "part of themselves" (1147a23) While able to "string together the phrases" of the craft the apprentice is often unable to apply those general principles to the range of concrete situations. The apprentice is unable reliably to recognize the relevant sorts of situation, and thereby to use those general principles in action. It is likely that the apprentice will

---

[1] Extolling the pure, chaste, vegetarian life.

characteristically lack the minor premise.

So far we have been reminded of the possibility of 'having and yet not having' knowledge in a very familiar sense; of the various aspects of practical knowledge which may be 'had yet not had'; and we have been provided with a diverse group of illustrations of cases where knowledge is 'had but not had', and that even though the agent claims to know. We do not yet have a precise account of the potential knowledge involved in akrasia, nor any more than a rough characterization of its explanation, viz. some alteration in bodily state due to the passions.

We should not expect more detail than this here. The first three passages are not <u>an account</u> of akrasia at all. Rather they are addressed (as Santas puts it) to the Socratic question "How is it <u>possible</u> for one to act contrary to his knowledge of what is best". But this is not an explanation of any akratic act.

> ...from the fact that a person's knowledge may be defective in any of these ways, it certainly does not follow that he will act contrary to it. He may act in accordance with it accidentally, or out of habit without realizing what he is doing, or simply may do nothing at all. To explain the incontinent action we need something in addition to not knowing in the full sense.[1]

The necessary additional factor is not introduced until the fourth passage. It is only here that Aristotle turns to provide the account of akrasia. A certain amount of speculative reconstruction is unavoidable;

---

[1] Gerasimos Santas, "Aristotle on Practical Inference, the Explanation of Action, and Akrasia", <u>Phronesis</u>, Vol. XIV, No. 2, 1969, p. 182.

the text here is even more fragmentary than the parts we have previously considered. Nonetheless it seems most plausible to read this fourth passage as providing a Socratic account of akrasia. The apparatus developed in the foregoing passages is invoked, then supplemented to provide the complete account.[1] There are two critical questions to consider about Aristotle's final account: a) what does he say about the syllogism(s) of the akrates in this passage, and b) how are these facts about the syllogisms, whatever they are, supposed to explain the akratic act.

---

The fragmentary character of the text, of course, provides ample foothold for those who would prefer to interpret Aristotle in an anti-Socratic fashion. Walsh details a variety of arguments designed to "divide the analysis...into a 'real' [anti-Socratic] and a less 'real' [quasi-Socratic] doctrine aimed only at some special audience", viz. the Academy. If one were to take Aristotle's account to be anti-Socratic, it would have to not depend heavily on some notion of potential knowledge, and there would be no reason for him to discount the protestations of the akrates as being not evidence of actual knowledge. Thus, if Aristotle's account were anti-Socratic, it would have to be contained in the fourth section alone, and that passage would have to supercede the previous ones where much was made of precisely these objectionable notions. This interpretation is not impossible; but it is much less plausible than the Socratic one set out here. It is much less plausible for at least the following reasons.
Aristotle's silence on the relation of the passages lends more support to an interpretation which sees them as a continuously developing account than to one which takes them to be two incompatible accounts. In making each of the first three points Aristotle refers to akrasia, with the suggestion that each should contribute to a complete explanation (1146b33, 1147a8, 15-20). At no point does he disavow their relevance. Moreover the fourth passage mentions each of the points considered in each of the three previous sections: the practical syllogism figures crucially (1147a25-33); some part of it is either not known, or not known 'in a full sense' (1147b6-12); and the analogy with persons mad, asleep or drunk is reiterated (1147b12). Thus, I think it is most plausible to expect a sort of Socratic position in the fourth passage.

b. The practical syllogism and the account of akrasia.

Aristotle first reiterates a doctrine about the practical syllogism that many have found difficult. When a person completes a practical syllogism she/he must immediately act, if able and not prevented. (In the De Motu he says that the conclusion is an action). In normal circumstances there is no distinction between 'completing' a practical syllogism and acting on that syllogism. Aristotle seems to leave no place for either a 'judgment' that this act is to be done, or a 'decision' to do it. The practical syllogism, as it were, connects the reasoning to action in one fell swoop.

Now the akrates performs the akratic act, and does not perform the continent (better) act. Thus it would seem that the akratic syllogism is complete, the syllogism of the good not complete. Aristotle attributes to the akrates a) a universal opinion "forbidding us to taste", a second universal opinion that "everything sweet is pleasant", and a particular premise that "this is sweet". Schematically, Aristotle attributes a completed akratic syllogism:

    P1  Everything sweet is pleasant (and ought to be tasted).
    p1  This is sweet.
    C1  Tastes this.

The syllogism of the good, by contrast, is somehow incomplete:

    P2  Everything sweet is harmful (and ought to be avoided).
    p2  This is sweet.
    C2  Avoids tasting this.

Some part of the syllogism of the good is had 'only potentially' by the akrates at the time of action. It is in this sense that "the position that Socrates sought to establish actually seems to result".[1]

Exactly what goes wrong with the syllogism of the good is a much more vexed and difficult question. A favored candidate is the minor premise.

> Now the last premise being both an opinion about a perceptible object, and being what determines our actions, this a man either has not when he is in a state of passion, or has it in the sense in which having knowledge does not mean knowing but only talking, as a drunken man may mutter the verses of Empedocles. (1147b8-12)

The minor premise is the last of two in setting out practical syllogisms; the preparatory discussion at 1146b35-1147a10 emphasized not having or not exercising knowledge of the minor; and the minor premise is an 'opinion about a perceptible object' (1147b8).

There is, however, a difficulty with this interpretation that has troubled many commentators. Consider the syllogisms set out on p.199. If the minor premise is lost from the syllogism of the good it seems <u>also</u> unavailable for the syllogism of the pleasant. But all the elements of the syllogism of the pleasant <u>must be</u> explicit and available to the akrates, since it is alleged to be the syllogism upon which the akrates acts. Thus, if both syllogisms involve the same minor premise, the minor premise of the <u>prohairesis</u> syllogism, it seems, cannot be lost, on pain of having no completed syllogism at all, and hence no action.

---

[1] Interpreters who would find an anti-Socratic view in this passage have, of course, reconstructed the syllogisms differently. While the particular details about the syllogisms are surely obscure enough in the text, Aristotle's insistence on <u>some</u> sort of failure in the syllogism of the good is clear. (c.f. 1147b6-12)

> ...for Aristotle's theory to work out it is necessary that whatever goes wrong in the practical reason-wish motivation must leave the other motivation intact (the same thing must not go wrong there), for the latter motivation is needed to explain the action.[1]

This difficulty arises only if the description under which certain foods are proscribed in the syllogism of the good is the same as the description under which they are recommended in the syllogism of the pleasant. The vast majority of commentators seem to believe that this is the obvious reading of the good major premise.[2] Aristotle does not, however, say what the good major premise is; he does not provide the description under which the dainty is forbidden. Thus, the following reconstruction, rather than that on p. 119 would seem possible:

    P1  Everything sweet is pleasant (and ought to be tasted).
    p1  This is sweet
    C1  Tastes this

and

    P3  Rich and creamy desserts are harmful (and ought to be avoided).
    p3  This is a rich and creamy dessert.
    C3  Avoids tasting this

The akrates could have p3 only potentially while yet having p1 actually; the syllogism of the pleasant could be intact although the syllogism of the good is not.

For some cases, no doubt, this solution works admirably -- the Lessing case for example, and the large class of cases where a reasonable

---

[1] Santas, "Aristotle", p. 183.

[2] c.f. Walsh, *Aristotle's Conception of Moral Weakness*, p. 106.

good major premise would proscribe only an excessive number of the acts in question. But it cannot be the general account: for a wide range of cases it is logically possible but psychologically quite mad to suppose that the different descriptions can be kept separate. It seems quite extraordinary, for example, to suppose that anyone could fail to know that rich and creamy desserts are also sweet. Thus, whenever it is appropriate to attribute P3 it seems equally appropriate to attribute P2, and the same difficulty arises. Loss of the minor premise cannot be a general solution.

The failure of this solution is not limited to such banal examples of akrasia either. Consider the student who is akratic with respect to taking out a loan. In this case the major premise of the akratic syllogism would be: P4. Going into debt is bad (and to be avoided). The major premise of the syllogism of the good would be: P5. Acquiring an adequate income on better than reasonable terms is good (and to be pursued). Now it is known to the student that the only way of acquiring an adequate income, under the circumstances, is to go into debt; indeed the crucial clause 'better than reasonable terms' belongs only to the context of lending and borrowing. Thus, whenever it is appropriate to attribute P5 it seems equally appropriate to attribute P6: Going into debt under these circumstances is good (and to be pursued). But the minor premise of this syllogism would be identical to the minor premise of the akratic syllogism. If it were lacking here, to explain the failure to go into debt, it would also be unavailable for the akratic syllogism.

There are two further difficulties with interpreting the minor premise to be the missing factor. At the conclusion of this discussion Aristotle says "it is not in the presence of what is thought to be knowledge proper that the affection of incontinence arises...but in that of perceptual knowledge" (1147b16-17). Now the minor premise seems to represent perceptual knowledge, and it is here asserted to be present, not absent, in akrasia. Secondly, not everything said about the 'last premise' (1147b8) is true of the minor premise. In particular, the minor premise *itself* is not "what determines our actions"; it does so only when combined with the major premise.

A second interpretation of the flaw is proposed by Santas, following Vlastos. Abandoning the minor premise, he suggests that the 'last premise' should be taken to refer to the *conclusion* of the syllogism of the good.[1] This view clearly avoids the risk of wrecking the syllogism needed for the akratic act. In addition it makes better sense of 1147a30-35; if the universal opinion is to 'forbid us to taste' and 'bid us avoid' the sweet, we must assume that a minor premise is present as well.

Despite these virtues the interpretation will not do. It does some violence to the text. But more seriously, the interpretation simply *reiterates* without explaining the failure to do the better. Obviously the conclusion of the syllogism of the good is absent; the

---

[1] Santas, "Aristotle", p. 183.

akrates does not do the better, and the conclusion is an action.

An ingenious third alternative has been suggested by Joachim. The akrates <u>fails to connect</u> the minor premise with the major premise of the good. This interpretation is indifferent between the various possible reconstructions of the syllogism of the good. Even if the description under which the act is forbidden is the same as that under which it is found attractive, the akratic syllogism is not wrecked by the failure to complete the <u>prohairesis</u> syllogism. The minor premise is not missing, it is merely misconnected. Joachim's language is colorful: the akrates fails to make a "vital connection" between the premises; the major premise fails to "fuse and coalesce" with the minor; the akrates lacks a "vivid and full consciousness of this percept as a case of the universal". That is, the akrates does not see that the principle embodied in the <u>prohairesis</u> major premise applies to the current situation, and forbids the act she/he is about to engage in. "The ignorance itself...is not the momentary presence of the false belief that the act is right, but the momentary absence of the true belief that the act is wrong."[1] For the akrates the question of what it is best to do in the situation <u>does not arise</u> at the time of action.

This interpretation may seem little more explanatory than Santas'. Walsh rejects it, saying that "this only amounts to a psychologized

---

[1] H. H. Joachim, <u>Aristotle, the Nicomachean Ethics, A Commentary</u>, ed. D. A. Rees (Oxford: The Clarendon Press, 1951); Reginald Jackson, "Rationalism and Intellectualism in the Ethics of Aristotle", <u>Mind</u>, Vol. LI, No. 204 (Oct. 1942), p. 352.

way of saying that the akrates does not draw the conclusion, does not act".[1] But it is a little more than that. Combining the premises is a sufficient condition for the conclusion (action) in normal circumstances, but it is not the same as the action. One may, for example, combine the premises and yet not act because one is unable to act or prevented from acting. Thus, Joachim's suggestion is somewhat better off than Santas'. It has, however, a rather ad hoc quality; and it gives us no direction for interpreting the passages which say that some item of knowledge becomes unavailable.

In sum then: Aristotle insists that akrasia is due to some temporary failure in the practical knowledge of the akrates. The particular failure is located in the practical syllogism of the good. There is no single account of precisely what goes wrong with that syllogism, which is both reasonable and consistent with everything Aristotle says about it. It is also not yet clear exactly how syllogisms function in the general explanation of action, and thus in the particular account of akrasia. In order to consider these matters, and flesh out the account in Book VII, we must place it within this more general context.

B. EN VII in Perspective

Aristotle's general theory of the explanation of action is of a piece with the functional account described in Chapter IV.

---

[1] James J. Walsh, Aristotle's Conception of Moral Weakness, p. 108. Columbia University Press, 1973, p. 108.

## 1. Aristotle and final causes

In the <u>De Anima</u> Aristotle defines soul as a "substance in the sense of the form of a body having life potentially in it" (412a20). The study of the soul is the study of what is in some sense an explanatory principle of the activities of living things (DA402a5). The sense in which soul is an explanatory principle is thus as a formal principle; an account of the soul is an account of the living body formally described. (c.f. <u>Metaphysics</u> 1036b20 & 1035a7) A formal principle, in turn, describes 'that for the sake of which' the activities of the body take place'. (<u>Physics</u> 199a33)

These claims about the soul (and psychological explanation) direct us to the <u>Physics</u>, where Aristotle sets out the general doctrine of the 'four causes', better rendered 'four sorts of explanation'. Aristotle was the first to articulate clearly these separate, complimentary, kinds of explanation that may legitimately interest us, of which we have been discussing two. "As the word has several senses it follows that there are several causes of the same thing" (195a3). He contrasts functional explanation with ordinary causal explanation in terms similar to those we employed above. Causal explanation points to the past: "the result is determined by antecedents" (200a13). Functional explanation makes reference to the future: "'That for the sake of which' means what is best and the end of the things that lead up to it" (195a22-27). Such explanation shows how means-events are necessary "on a hypothesis" (200a13); it explains the means-events by reference to the end, and not the end itself.

> The same completion is not reached from every principle, nor any chance completion, but always the tendency in each is toward the same end, if there is no impediment. (199b17)

Non-achievement of the end is to be explained in terms of 'an impediment', 'a corruption', or 'failure' in the normal sequence of means events.

Aristotle does not elaborate on how the general theory of functional explanation is to be adapted to account for special complexities in the case of conscious functional systems. In the <u>De Anima</u>, after extremely general points about the soul as the form of the body, we find him just introducing 'sensation', 'thinking' and 'desire' (DA413b10-23). A welcome supplement to these remarks, however, is to be found in the theory of deliberation in the <u>Nicomachean Ethics</u>.

Practical reasoning consists in figuring out the best way, within ones power, of attaining some end that one has adopted. "The man who is deliberating is searching for something and calculating" (1142b15). Taking an end as given, persons deliberate about "how and by what means it is to be attained" (1144d7). A person considers sometimes the instrument, sometimes the use of them until she/he has brought the moving principle back to [her] himself. In the <u>Metaphysics</u>, Aristotle provides an example of the steps such a process of thinking might involve. The doctor's end is to make the patient healthy. He considers how that will be achieved in this case. Health here will be produced by making the humors balanced. How is that to be achieved? By increasing the body heat. How is that to be achieved? By rubbing the skin. Here at last is something "within the power" of the doctor; the "starting point" of action. (<u>Metaphysics</u> 1032b15-25)

As an account of the actual thought processes a person goes through each time she/he acts purposefully, this picture is, of course, baroque. However, the theory might be construed rather as indicating the structure reasons must take if purposive behaviour is to be explained and sometimes justified.[1]

Aristotle's examples of practical reasoning usually involve technical, or professional, deliberation; the thinking involved in the doctor's production of health, or the general's production of victory. Nonetheless, it is clear that he intends the pattern exhibited in these examples to apply to practical reasoning generally. Difficulties arise in trying to work out such an application which are not essential to our purposes here. What is essential is that in general practical reasoning, involves a 'search', but one that is more complicated than that involved in technical deliberation. Not only may there be alternative means to a given end, but man qua moral being, unlike man qua doctor, has a multiplicity of ends, and some of these ends may conflict. Aristotle has said that deliberation is about means and not about ends. How, then, can the theory apply to cases of conflict; how can deliberation resolve conflict?

An examination of Aristotle's notion of 'means' and 'end' provides the answer. The Greek word translated 'means' has a rather broader sense that the English indicates; a better translation for general practice contexts would be something like "things that contribute to, or

---

[1] John Cooper, <u>Reason and Human Good in Aristotle</u> (Cambridge: Harvard University Press, 1975).

promote, or have a positive bearing on". Secondly, an 'end' for Aristotle is something desired for its own sake and not (merely) as a means to something else; men clearly have a variety of ends in this sense. Each of these ends, when treated as an end, cannot be deliberated about. But many such ends are pursued both for their own sakes (e.g. good tasty food) <u>and also</u> for the sake of something else (viz. nourishment and health). When considered as a means to some other end they can be deliberated about. Aristotle argues that a person's ends are, or ought to be, hierarchically ordered. It is fine to seek good, tasty food <u>unless</u> that food is harmful to health. The end of health takes, or ought to take precedence over the end of pleasure at table. Furthermore, they are, or ought to be, hierarchically ordered in the strongest possible way, with one single end taking precedence over all others. "We must enjoin everyone...to set up for himself some object for the beautiful life to aim at, with reference to which he will then do all his acts, since not to have one's life organized in view of some end is a mark of great folly"(EE1214b8-11). That one has an Ultimate End does not prevent one's pursuing other things also as ends, but each of these ends must also be a means to the Ultimate End. Aristotle's examples of deliberation all begin with ends that are subordinate in this sense. However, a deliberative examination of these ends is by no means ruled out on his account; indeed the hierarchical structure he is at pains to defend requires that such an examination should be possible. (c.f. 1142b30). Because ends have this structure, resolution of conflict by rational decision is always possible. Only the Ultimate

End is not subject to the kind of explanation, and justification deliberation can provide.

Given this general account of the structure of deliberation and action explanation, how does the practical syllogism figure in it? It is clearly not a general model for deliberation.[1] Many of the characteristics essential to practical syllogisms are simply absent from deliberation. At no point does deliberation depend on particulars; the same considerations would apply to any patient similarly afflicted; the conclusion of deliberation is a general description of a kind of action. Deliberation, it seems, must be complete before we can have the <u>major premise</u> of a practical syllogism. There may be alternative ways of making the patient healthy; the doctor is searching for the best way. Practical syllogisms are no use for this purpose, as Davidson points out. Finally the doctor may be deliberating late at night in his study, and he can conclude his deliberation there, far from the context of action. The conclusion of a syllogism, by contract, <u>is</u> an action.

What role, then, does the practical syllogism serve? The major premise in Aristotle's examples normally specifies a kind of action which is 'within the power' of the agent -- e.g. taste this, avoid tasting this. Thus no further thinking is required to 'bring the starting point back to himself'. All that is required at this

---

[1]This point is so obvious I am at a loss to explain the number of commentators that make it so. Davidson, "How is Weakness of Will Possible?", pp. 102-3.

point is <u>recognition</u> that circumstances are ripe for realization of the end. John Cooper has suggested that the practical syllogism is simply a way of making explicit the contribution of perception to action after deliberation is already complete.[1] The practical syllogism spells out an essential <u>background</u> condition of an action in accord with a particular deliberative conclusion. The role of the syllogism in action explanation would then be the way of specifying what the agent intended to do, i.e. what <u>action</u> was actually performed. Taking the syllogism discussed in Book VII, a single bodily movement -- the hand reaching for the chocolate eclair -- might be viewed either under the description 'tasting something pleasant' or 'doing something harmful to health', or both. Citing the practical syllogism(s) <u>actually</u> involved in the action would indicate where explanation should begin, by showing what action was performed.

2. The place of potential knowledge

Aristotle insists in VII that when a person acts, intentionally, contrary to her/his better judgment, it must be the case that that person is, at the time, aware only 'potentially' of the fact that that act is contrary to her/his higher ranking aims (goals). The akrates is not 'actually' aware of this fact. Rather, she/he is 'actually' aware only of another, compatible fact about the situation, viz. that there is, after all, <u>something</u> to be said for tasting the sweet, staying in bed, boarding the plane, or whatever. Aristotle expresses

---

[1] John Cooper, <u>Reason</u>

these perceptions and failures of perception, in the language of practical syllogisms. The syllogism of the good, he says, is fragmented, incomplete. The syllogism of the pleasant (or some other akratic x) only is intact.

At least two elements in this account of akrasia are striking. The first is simply the emphasis on practical syllogisms. The details of the syllogism, and various malformations to which it is subject preoccupy Aristotle here; the syllogism figures crucially in his final account. In other parts of the *Ethics*, where he is concerned with more general issues in the explanation of action, practical syllogisms are strikingly absent.

The second striking feature is Aristotle's passing the explanatory buck at a certain point. If we want to know how the syllogism of the good became fragmented, and how the eyes of the akrates are later re-opened to what she/he has done, he says that we should consult the 'natural scientist' and not the philosopher. Why does Aristotle focus sharply on the syllogism here; what job does he relegate to the natural scientist?

Both moves, I suggest, indicate that the explanation of akrasia will be significantly different from the explanation of a normal case of action; moreover, they indicate something crucial about the particular nature of the difference.

If, as seems plausible, there is no way to render open-eyed akrasia compatible with a functional account of the explanation of action, then akrasia cannot be accounted for as any kind of normal functioning.

An account of it must be different from an account of the normal case. The role assigned to both the practical syllogism and to the natural scientist in the explanation of akrasia support this. Both moves indicate that at least a part of the explanation of akrasia will be an explanation not in terms of final causes but rather in terms of efficient causes.

> Intentional explanation and prediction cannot be accommodated either to breakdown or to less than optimal design, so there is no coherent Intentional description of such an impasse... It is from the physical stance alone that we can predict the malfunction of systems.[1]

The Intentional system that is the akrates has thus 'broken down' in some sense, but it has not 'broken down' entirely. The akrates does, after all, act intentionally. The details of the Book VII account follow the standard pattern for the explanation of breakdowns in functional systems; further the details account for the particular nature of the akratic breakdown, viz. that what the akrates does, she/he does intentionally.[2]

This interpretation is supported by noting the characterization of akrasia with respect to Aristotle's theoretical notions of 'choice' and the 'voluntary'. The akrates acts, he says, 'contrary to choice', but yet 'voluntarily'. 'Choice, is the technical term which specifies the aims and purposes correctly attributable to individual agents. 'Voluntary' acts are those which proceed from the agent her/himself

---

[1] D. C. Dennett, "Intentional Systems", pp. 88, 104.

[2] Chapter IV, Section C (p.  )

and not, eg. from some external coercive agent, from disease processes, or from alcohol ingested. Actions in general are explained by exhibiting their contribution to the aims and purposes of the agent; they are not explained simply by locating the cause of the act within the agent her/himself. Thus, it is only rational action which is action in accordance with 'choice'. It is only rational action which is subject to the normal account. "In choice lies the essential element of virtue and character." "Choice is either desiderative reason or ratiocinative desire, and such an origin of action is a man." E.(1139b3-5) Only those actions are 'chosen' which express a person's character, by virtue of contributing to her/his ends. Thus, only action which is 'chosen' is subject to <u>normal</u> functional explanation. Akrasia is precisely not action which expresses a person's character; it is action contrary to whatever ends she/he has adopted; it is action contrary to 'choice'. Thus, akrasia is not subject to normal functional explanation. Akrasia is, however, 'voluntary'. As a kind of intentional action, we would expect the explanation to be an instance of some systemmatic modification of functional explanation.

Both parts of this task are precisely what the account in Book VII accomplishes. The insistance that some part of the akrates' practical knowledge is there 'only potentially' explains why there is this kind of non-normal functioning. And, it is precisely the, required, delicate delineation of <u>the kind</u> of non-normal functioning at issue that Aristotle accomplishes by the introduction of the practical syllogism. Akrasia is explained by being shown to be due to the interference of efficient causes of a very particular sort with the functional system of purposive behaviour.

3. Theoretical elegance of EN VII

In order to sharply exhibit Aristotle's strategy here, we must recall one formal feature of functional explanation. The feature of direct relevance is the assymmetry noted, regarding which sorts of events require what sort of explanation.

> That a system achieves its end state does not require or admit of further explanation [in functional terms]; but should it achieve any other result, we are bound to give an account. Abnormal functioning must bring in a set of laws linking interfering factors and non-normal conditions which are not teleological.[1]

Intentional explanation, we have argued, presupposes a wealth of background causal conditions. The environment must be felicitous, the person alive, awake, attending to the environment, possessed of a normal body and functioning nervous system. If these, and other, causally necessary background conditions did not obtain there simply would not be the phenomenon of intentional action to be explained at all. Intentional explanation presupposes these conditions; it does not refer to them. Mention of background conditions is not a part of the explanation of normal functioning. Such reference is, however, central to the explanation of abnormal functioning, and to complete breakdown of functioning. Thus, the explanation of akrasia, qua

---

[1] Charles Taylor, The Explanation of Behaviour, London: Routledge and Kegan Paul, 1964, p. 22.

abnormal functioning, requires reference to some failure in this normal background of necessary conditions.

Of course, not just any failure would result in a case of akrasia. Dead, sleeping or paralyzed persons are not, as it were, 'weak' when they fail to do the better. Clearly, there must be a particular sub-set of these background conditions, failure of certain members of which, while incompatible with an action's being 'chosen', is yet compatible with the person acting, and acting voluntarily. Indeed, it is precisely such actions, 'voluntary' but 'contrary to choice' that comprise the phenomenon of akrasia. Here the particular elegance of Aristotle's move, invoking practical syllogisms. The failure is the fragmentation of the syllogism of the good; however the akratic syllogism remains intact. Let us explicate further the place of the syllogisms here.

The practical syllogism is strikingly absent from Aristotle's discussion of action in general; it dominates the discussion of akrasia. Now we can see why. The minimal role of the syllogism in Aristotle's general theory of action was suggested to be that of making explicit the contribution of perception to the process of acting for reasons. It is a presupposition of action explanation that persons perceive accurately relevant facts of the situation they are in, just as it is a presupposition that they are alive, awake, have normal nervous systems, etc. Practical perception is a presupposition of the normal account; it is not a part of that account. Hence Aristotle's neglect of the practical syllogism in his general account of action. The background is forced to the foreground, however, in accounting for breakdowns. This particular element in the background is just the one Aristotle needs. Hence his preoccupation with the syllogism in Book VII.

That the syllogism of the good be fragmented is essential to explain why the akrates does not do what she/he believes, in some sense, it is best to do. The akrates does not do the better because a causally necessary pre-condition of this action is absent. The akrates does, however, act, and acts voluntarily. Providing a syllogism of the pleasant ensures the voluntariness of the action that is performed.

The account of akrasia is a subtle and powerful application of the general theory of syllogisms. According to Hardie, "the center of Aristotle's interest when he produces the doctrine [of the practical syllogism] is in the psychology, indeed the psychophysics, of action; in what happens in a man, in a besouled and mindful body, when, and immediately before, he initiates change".[1] When and immediately before a person acts intentionally, for a reason, she/he must perceive that this is some reasonable context in which to act for that reason. This 'perception', I suggest, is a causally necessary pre-condition for the person acting for that reason, that is, performing that intentional action. It is a causally necessary pre-condition for there being that action to be functionally explained.[2]

---

[1] W. F. R. Hardie, Aristotle's Ethical Theory; Oxford: The Clarendon Press, 1968; p. 248.

[2] "We must not, I hope it is clear, think that actions can simply be sorted into the incontinent [or the intentional] and others.

Aristotle's insistance that the akrates knows the syllogism of the good 'only potentially' at the time of action amounts to the claim that she/he is not viewing the action under the description 'worse, all things considered'. It is essential that this description be unavailable. If it were available, <u>that</u> perception would indicate the appropriate background condition to account only for the akrates <u>abstaining</u> from the action. The akratic act is possible because and only because the akrates, while having the correct beliefs, fails to <u>note</u> their relevance to the case at hand. It is this failure which explains the failure to act on these beliefs. It is this failure which explains the non-occurrence of the act/omission which would have been functionally explicable. This is the point of the analogy to persons "mad, asleep, or drunk". Each of these conditions is clearly a case of an impaired, or absent, ability to appreciate accurately the practical context. The sleeper fails to have any practical perceptions at all, while the perceptions of the drunk and the madman are characteristically distorted.

Aristotle does not explicitly discuss how the syllogism of the good gets obscured; he refers us to the natural scientist for an account of how it is recovered. Two of the above analogies can clarify this matter as well. In each of these cases there is a causal explanation, obtainable from the scientist, for the failure of perception. For

---

'Incontinent', like 'intentional', 'voluntary' and 'deliberate' characterize actions only as conceived in one way rather than another." Davidson, "How is Weakness of Will Possible?", p. 97.

the sleeper it is the physiological state of sleep; for the drunk it is the alcohol; for the akrates, it seems, it is a kind of unruly desire system. 'Passion' or 'appetite' blind the person. Further, in these cases (unlike most cases of madness) the cause of the blindness is a condition for which we are ourselves responsible. Just as the drunken person should not have gotten drunk, and Jesus' disciples should not have fallen asleep, so the akrates ought to have cultivated better habits.[1]

We have, to this point, provided an explanation for why the akrates does not do what she/he judges better; and also for why she/he is responsible for this failure. A further explanation is required for why she/he does, and does voluntarily, what she/he believes (in some sense of 'believes') to be the worse. It is this feature of voluntariness that distinguishes the akrates from persons who are "mad, asleep, or drunk", and from all the other unfortunate characters wrongly admitted on Davidson's account. It is this crucial feature that made the accounts of Anscombe and Cooper -- "she/he did it for the pleasure of it" -- initially attractive.

---

[1] 1143b11-14. "Therefore we ought to attend to the undemonstrated sayings and opinions of experienced and order people or people of practical wisdom not less than to demonstrations; for because experience has given them an eye they see aright"...
1113b30-34. "...we punish a man for his very ignorance if he is thought responsible for the ignorance, as when penalties are doubled in the case of drunkenness; for the moving principle is in the man himself, since he had the power of not getting drunk and his getting drunk was the cause of his ignorance."

This explanation is provided by Aristotle in attributing an akratic syllogism to the akrates. "The practical syllogism is...a scheme of logically necessary conditions for intentional action."[1] In attributing a weak syllogism to the akrates, Aristotle indicates that the action is seen under a reasonable description. That an act satisfies some description such as this -- is pleasant, is socially graceful, etc. -- may well provide good reason for doing it, other things equal. The akrates may well even do what she/he thinks best -- thinks best, that is, minus a few crucial beliefs. That is, minus the belief that the act is worse overall, an akratic act may well accord with her/his remaining moral or prudential priorities. The belief that the act is worse over-all is precisely what has been lost with the fragmentation of the good syllogism. There is thus produced the temporary illusion that other things are equal. The force of the akratic reason is appreciated in splendid isolation from other, conflicting, reasons.

Mention of the weak syllogism is thus a necessary but insufficient part of a complete explanation of akrasia. It is necessary, in order to ensure that the akratic act is itself intentional; it is insufficient for two reasons. Firstly, syllogisms themselves do not explain actions. Rather, they fix the correct description for the act. The act itself, under that description, is then explained in the

---

[1] Mary Mothersill, "Anscombe's Account of the Practical Syllogism", The Philosophical Review, Vol. LXXI, No. 4, (Oct. 1962), pp. 448-461.

normal way, by being related to the aims and purposes of the agent overall. Secondly, an act under an akratic description <u>can be</u> so explained only on condition that the considerations which underly the syllogism of the good are not brought to bear.

A modification of occurrent beliefs is a standard first move used by any action theorist to account for apparent irrationality, when a person nonetheless appears to be acting intentionally. Reflection on how Aristotle's account of akrasia is constructed illuminates why this move is rightly attractive, and why it is in fact powerful. The move works not because it locates correctly the cause of the act, as Goldman and Hempel claim. Rather, it functions by calling attention to certain background conditions which are claimed to be non-normal. Appeal to this particular abnormality is attractive, when defensible for at least two reasons. We can explain the (irrational) act that was performed with a minimal dislocation of the explanatory framework. And the particular nature of the dislocation is compatible with the intentionality of the act that was performed.

### C. Concluding Remarks

Thus, Aristotle's account of akrasia represents a theoretically elegant solution to the problem akrasia poses for the best general theory of action explanation. It requires the denial of open-eyed akrasia, but provides an explanation of a phenomenon described as the skeptic would have it. No account of open-eyed akrasia has yet been proposed which is compatible with a reasonable general theory. This fact alone provides strong reason to side with the skeptics, at least for the present, and to accept Aristotle's account. But it would be desirable to do more.

It would be desirable to show, in addition, that Aristotle's view is able to handle some of the most pressing objections that have been leveled against it. And it would be desirable to provide an explanation for the other, conflicting, believers side of our intuitions. It is to this further task that we now turn. The two parts of the task overlap to some extent. Some of the objections arise from mere misunderstanding; when this is the case the misunderstanding itself sometimes explains the believer's intuition.

1. Defence against objections

First, a minor textual difficulty. There is no single, coherent account in EN VII of precisely what goes wrong with the syllogism of the good. Some philosophers have found this problem to be dire.[1] It becomes quite insignificant, by contrast, given our interpretation of syllogisms. Since the syllogism does not represent a process run through at all, there is no need to say precisely where the process is interrupted. When Aristotle says that the syllogism of the good is fragmented, incomplete, this simply amounts to the claim that that description does not apply to the act. The logical scheme as a whole is denied application.

---

[1] Santas, "Aristotle", p. 175.

Surely the most pressing objection to Aristotle and any other skeptic is the requirement that we override the testimony of numerous akrateis themselves. Many insist that they did know full well that the act was for the worse; they suffered no temporary ignorance. Davidson insists that he judged it better to remain in bed, Dostoyevsky alludes to millions more. Agents themselves often resist such high-handed treatment of their first-person reports in the name of over-bearing theory; and there is philosophical support for their stubbornness.[1]

This objection must first be clarified. It is not plausible that the skeptic overrides nearly as many first-person reports nearly as often as Davidson and Dostoyevsky make it seem. We have already seen that the Underground Man is confused in thinking he disagrees with the skeptic at all. How careful have the other objectors been? Sidgewick is one known for careful introspection. He notes, rather charmingly, "some difficulty in observing cases of ones own willful wrong-doing". Akrasia belongs, he suggests, to "a class of phenomena which tend to be prevented by attempts to direct ones attention to them". (This feature is "practically advantageous, but inconvenient from a scientific point of view").[2] If this is what Sidgwick found,

---

[1] See for example Richard Rorty, "Incorrigibility as the Mark of the Mental", Journal of Philosophy, Vol. LXVII, No. 12, (June 25, 1970), pp. 399-424. Incorrigibility is not claimed for all first person reports, but it is defended in the case of mental events, such as an occurrent judgment is understood to be.

[2] Henry Sidgewick, "Unreasonable Action!", p. 174.

how are we to explain the strong popular resistance to the skeptic? Just how much first person testimony does the skeptic override?

We might plausibly explain a good deal of the popular resistance in terms of an unnoticed equivocation -- or better, several unnoticed equivocations. The skeptic does not override first person reports if the claim the skeptic denies is a claim <u>other than</u> (albeit related to) the claim the resistant akrates is concerned to maintain. There are several obvious candidates for claims an akrates might well be concerned to defend which do not in fact conflict with anything the skeptic wishes to assert. These are alternative, compatible, independently sufficient ways of answering the objection. In each of these cases no first person testimony is really overridden.

First, a resistant akrates may have not attended carefully to the specific content of the judgment at issue. In the case of the fleshly forms of akrasia a reasonable judgment might well proscribe only certain <u>practices</u> -- such as being a smoker, or being one given to overeating. The reasons that proscribe the practice often do not apply to any particular, individual, act of smoking or eating. Thus, one might well judge that one ought not to be a smoker, or one given to overeating, and yet not judge that one ought not to smoke the very cigarette now being offered to one. If one judges only the former, and not the latter, the skeptic does not deny anything this akrates wants to maintain, for the skeptic insists that one judge only potentially that the act one performs is for the worse. (Of course the practice is not something other than acts of that sort performed with a not very definite frequency; but it is certainly to be distinguished from any particular act).

Other resistant akrateis may want to insist that they know <u>in general</u> that certain of their actions are for the worse. In general they are able to recognize situations in which, eg. eating too much or smoking too much is at issue. They are neither stupid nor constitutionally blind. The Aristotelian of course does not deny this either. Indeed, the skeptic insists that one must have this ability regarding such matters if one is to be able to suffer akrasia in this area. It is not the general ability to recognize that the skeptic denies, but only the <u>occurrent</u> awareness, at the time of action, -- the awareness which would be a causally necessary background condition of doing the worse intentionally.

These alternatives would probably resolve some but only some of the original conflicts. What of the remaining sub-set of originally resistant akrateis -- those who politely refuse these attempts at negotiation? They may well grant that our suggestions cover some cases, but insist that there are also others. There are also cases where the judgment they made cannot be reinterpreted in either of these conciliatory fashions. Is it even possible that the skeptic be right and the akrates wrong in such a case?

Once again, there are several alternatives open to the skeptic. Let us trace out first the possibilities with respect to the judgment of the akrates, and then trace another path of replies.

It is neither impossible, nor even very implausible to suppose that the akrates has simply remembered wrong. No one concerned to defend the special epistemological status of first-person reports of their mental life is concerned to credit very highly the accurracy of <u>memories</u> of what one said or did, much less judged, sometime in the past. Indeed, it is for the most part only headstrong persons, or persons with some special axe to grind about a particular incident, that even strongly resist having their seeming memories argued to be mistaken, if good reason is provided to think that they are wrong. The temptation to introspect, and introspect again, in order to certify that one did judge the akratic act to be the worse at the very instant of performing it, is no more likely to yield the truth of the matter than is buying several copies of the morning paper likely to assure one that what it says is true. Returning in memory or imagination to the moment of ones weakness is not returning to the moment of ones weakness.

But suppose that an akrates (perhaps a Humean determined to prove us wrong) were to perform an akratic act <u>right now</u>, before our very eyes. What if such an akrates were to insist, "You see, I <u>do</u> realize, right now, this instant, that this is a cigarette, smoking <u>this</u> cigarette is the worse (perhaps it is the one which will spark off my dormant habit again). And yet I smoke it. I am actually aware of that right now! How can you, skeptic, possibly deny it??"

It would not be entirely unreasonable for the skeptic to suspect that this is not an akratic act at all (at least on this occasion), but rather one judged best under the circumstances. She/he might well suspect that the (alleged) akrates thought it more important ('better') to disprove this bad theory than to avoid the damage done by one cigarette. (In splendid isolation, of course, no cigarette is worthy of much practical notice). If these suspicions are correct the skeptic's theory is no more disproven than is determinism by the out-of-character antics sometimes engaged in by over-zealous indeterminists. If even the behaviour of the Underground Man is compatible with the skeptic's claims about akrasia that theory surely can handle one cigarette.

This reply, though attractive, is not decisive. It would be dogmatic and unreasonable for the skeptic to <u>insist</u> that <u>every</u> time an akrates is, as it were, caught in the act, and reports that they are aware <u>just now</u> that the act they are performing just now is the worse, that the apparent counter-instance can be explained away in this fashion. It is still possible, however, to avoid a head-on conflict of first-person reports and consequences of the skeptic's account without recourse to such dogmatism.

First, and most importantly, an occurrent judgment that an act is, all things considered, the worse is but one of several conditions set out in defining open-eyed akrasia. The skeptic's claim that there is no phenomena answering to that description requires only a <u>conditional</u> statement in this dispute with resistant akrates. All the skeptic need insist is that <u>if</u> the act is strongly intentional, and there are no unconscious motivations at work, and the real reason is the akratic reason <u>simpliciter</u>, and the agent could have done otherwise, <u>then</u> the akrates does not also judge occurrently that the akratic act is worse, all things considered. Now these other conditions are very far from being reasonable candidates (if any mental states are) for being incorrigible, indubitable to the agent. As we noted in Chapter I, neither we nor the agent can be certain, in any particular case, that these conditions obtain. That is one reason the believers could not short-cut this whole investigation simply by producing a case of open-eyed akrasia. In the face of the adamant insistence of an akrates who claims to judge (occurrently), the skeptic also has the option of altering instead one of these other conditions: she/he need only deny that <u>all</u> these conditions can obtain together.

This is surely a very common reason that the bare bones of the skeptic's account tends to be strongly resisted, and once again it rests on a confusion. On the one hand the skeptic's account is thought strongly counter-intuitive; on the other hand, our thinking about actual cases turns out to be strikingly Socratic -- though usually by altering one of these other conditions. We tend, as with Lessing, to posit an unconscious motivation; or, as with the Underground Man, to recommend (surreptitiously) some other account of the (really) best thing to do; or we suggest, as with Praisegod Peipsum, that we couldn't, really, help it, we couldn't really have done otherwise.

Thus, it seems that there is no real life case in which a skeptic would feel theory-bound to ride roughshod over first-person reports of what they are occurrently aware of. But what of the theoretically possible case? What of the case where ex hypothesi we have good reason to believe that all these other conditions are satisfied, and yet the person acts akratically and claims to realize that it is the worse while in the very process of performing the akratic act? The Aristotelian approach to mental states is relevant here, no less than to attributing the other conditions. Mental states in general are theoretical states introduced to explain behaviour. Different kinds of states succeed in explaining different behaviours. There is surely a difference between practical judgment on the one hand, and having thoughts or entertaining ideas on the other. In this theoretically possible case it would seem not unreasonable to countenance the need to override the claims of the akrates to judge, in the name of theory, and to attribute instead the 'mere thought' that the act was the worse.

The skeptic has, it seems, successfully avoided this battery of attempts to falsify the account of akrasia. But has not the skeptic too, no less than the want theorist, escaped the Scylla of falsity only to founder on the Charybdis of vacuity? Has not the skeptic's account of akraisa become trivially true because quite obviously circular? If ever the skeptic is faced with strong reason to think an alleged akrates does judge occurrently that the act is the worse, she/he merely slides away, denying one of the other conditions of akrasia, on which she/he is even less easily faulted.

The skeptic would do well to admit straightaway to the circularity of the account. Indeed, she/he might insist that the circularity of the interlocking specifications is no accident. This circle, however, unlike the want theorist's is virtuous rather than vicious; it may claim this virtue in virtue of its large diameter. The significant fact about our thinking about the whole cluster of pre-theoretic cases, and the various moves we make to ease various sorts of theoretical strain, is precisely this fact. All these features in our understanding and explanation of action are in fact deeply and irrevocably interconnected. It is this interconnection that the skeptic's account stubbornly holds fast to -- and that has been illuminated by coming to an understanding of that account, and showing the respects in which it is superiour to its competitors.

## 2. In retrospect

We have been examining the ancient debate over the possibility of open-eyed akrasia, from the point of view of theory of action, and that of our (surprisingly) ambivalent intuitions. At first glance it appeared that nearly everyone believes that there is such a thing as open-eyed akrasia, in addition to whatever other varieties of unreasonable action. Socrates' contrary claim, that akrasia "is nothing but ignorance and mastery of oneself is nothing but wisdom" appeared very implausible. Common sense is no guarantee of truth in such matters, but it is, in this case, backed up by a respectable array of philosophical arguments. In particular, there are numerous accounts of akrasia which offer to show that open-eyed akrasia is in fact compatible with reasonable general beliefs about action.

We have considered in detail two of the best accounts of open-eyed akrasia yet proposed. In Chapter II we considered a Platonic/Humean and currently popular account in terms of strength of desire. In Chapter III we considered a subtle and difficult account recently proposed by Davidson, exploiting the general doctrines of token materialism and the anomalousness of the mental. Both accounts proved seriously flawed. In each case the account of akrasia itself was problemmatic. Though compatible with their respective general theories, each in its own way failed to preserve certain crucial features of akrasia as normally understood. More seriously, both general frameworks for theory of action were argued to be inadequate --each for different reasons.

In Chapter IV we turned to articulate a better theoretical framework, one which was argued to be found in Aristotle. We then considered a variety of attempts to render open-eyed akrasia compatible with this best general theory. Once again these attempts proved unsucessful. Each attempt to make a place for akrasia within the scheme opened a Pandora's box of implausible cases which slipped in under the same conditions. No account yet proposed enables us to delimit in a reasonable fashion the sort of irrational cases admitted. It is possible, of course, that a better account will be proposed in the future. But at this point it seemed only reasonable to consider the force of the opposing, skeptic's, case.

We traced first the theoretical elegance of Aristotle's account of akrasia within the framswork of the best general theory. Aristotle's account makes room for akrasia with a minimal dislocation of the explanatory scheme. These theoretical considerations provided some reason to force some recalcitrant data into line, should that prove necessary. Upon closer examination, however, it turned out that remarkably little such violence was in fact required. Very many objections to Aristotle's version of a skeptical account of akrasia turned on misunderstanding; those that remained seemed a not unreasonable price to pay for an otherwise admirable account. These strengths should be sufficient to persuade us that akrasia may well exist only in the Socratic variety; they may even be sufficient to persuade us that it does.

SELECTED BIBLIOGRAPHY

Abelson, Raziel. "Doing, Causing, and Causing to Do". Review of Richard Taylor's Action and Purpose. The Journal of Philosophy. Vol. LXVI No. 6 (March 27, 1969): 178-192.

Anscombe, G.E.M. Intention. Oxford: Basil Blackwell, 1957.

_____. "Thought and Action in Aristotle". New Essays on Plato and Aristotle. Edited by Renford Bambrough. London: Routledge and Kegan Paul, 1965.

Aristotle. De Anima. Translated by J.A. Smith. The Works of Aristotle Translated into English, Vol. III. Edited by W.D. Ross. Oxford: Clarendon Press, 1931.

_____. Ethica Nicomachea. Translated by W.D. Ross. The Works of Aristotle Translated into English, Vol. IX. Edited by W.D. Ross. Oxford: Clarendon Press, 1931.

_____. Physica. Translated by R.P. Hardie and R.K. Gaye. The Works of Aristotle Translated into English, Vol. II. Edited by W.D. Ross. Oxford: Clarendon Press, 1931.

Austin, John. "A Plea for Excuses". Proceedings of the Aristotelian Society. Vol. LVII (1956/7).

Berofsky, Bernard. "Purposive Action". American Philosophical Quarterly. Vol. VII, No. 4 (Oct. 1970): 311-320.

Brandt, Richard. "Traits of Character: A Conceptual Analysis". American Philosophical Quarterly. Vol. VII, No. 1 (January 1970): 23-37.

Brown, D.G. Action. London: George Allen and Unwin Ltd., 1968.

Chisholm, Roderick. "The Structure of Intention". The Journal of Philosophy. Vol. LXVII, No. 19 (Oct. 8, 1970): 633-647.

Cooper, John. Reason and Human Good in Aristotle. Cambridge: Harvard University Press, 1975.

Cooper, Neil. "Oughts and Wants". In Weakness of Will. Edited by G.W. Mortimore. London: Macmillan, St. Martin's Press, 1971.

Davidson, Donald. "Actions, Reasons, and Causes". In Readings in the Theory of Action. Edited by Norman S. Care and Charles Landesman. Bloomington: Indiana University Press, 1968.

_____. "Freedom to Act". In Essays on Freedom of Action. Edited by Ted Honderich. London: Routledge and Kegan Paul, 1973.

_____. "How is Weakness of Will Possible?" In Moral Concepts. Edited by Joel Feinberg. London: Oxford University Press, 1969.

_____. "Mental Events". In Experience and Theory. Edited by Lawrence Foster and J.W. Swanson. Amherst: University of Massachusetts Press, 1970.

Dennett, D.C. Content and Consciousness. London: Routledge and Kegan Paul, 1969.

_____. "Intentional Systems". The Journal of Philosophy. Vol. LXVIII, No. 4. (February 25, 1971): 87-106.

Dray, William. Laws and Explanations in History. Oxford: Oxford University Press, 1957.

Dostoyevsky, Fodor. Notes from Underground. Translated by Jesse Coulson. London: Penguin Classics, 1972.

Goldman, Alvin. A Theory of Human Action. Englewood Cliffs, New Jersey: Prentice-Hall, Inc. 1970.

Goodman, Nelson. "Seven Strictures on Similarity". In Experience and Theory. Edited by Lawrence Foster and J.W. Swanson. Amherst: University of Massachusetts Press, 1970.

Grice, Paul. "Probability, Desirability, and Mood Operators". Unpublished paper.

Hampshire, Stuart. Thought and Action. London: Chatto and Windus, 1959.

Hardie, W.F.R. Aristotle's Ethical Theory. Oxford: The Clarendon Press, 1968.

Hare, R.M. Freedom and Reason. Oxford: Clarendon Press, 1963.

Harman, Gilbert. "Davidson on How Weakness of Will is Possible". Unpublished paper.

Hempel, Carl G. Aspects of Scientific Explanation. New York: The Free Press, 1965.

Hume, David. A Treatise of Human Nature. In two volumes. Edited by
A.D. Lindsay. London: Dent, Everyman's Library, 1966.

Jackson, Reginald. "Rationalism and Intellectualism in the Ethics of
Aristotle". Mind. Vol. LI No. 204 (October 1942): 343-360.

Joachim, H.H. Aristotle, The Nicomachean Ethics, A Commentary. Edited
by D.A. Rees. Oxford: The Clarendon Press, 1951.

Kuhn, Thomas. The Structure of Scientific Revolutions. Chicago:
University of Chicago Press, 1962.

Lessing, Doris. The Golden Notebook. New York: Ballentine Books,
Simon and Schuster, Inc.,1962.

Malcolm, Norman. "The Conceivability of Mechanism". The Philosophical
Review. Vol. LXXVII, No. 4 (1968): 63-72.

Mann, Thomas. "The Way to the Churchyard". In Stories of Three Decades.
Translated by H.T. Lowe-porter. New York: Alfred Knopf, 1936.

Melden, A.I. Free Action. London: Routledge and Kegan Paul Ltd. 1961.

Mothersill, Mary. "Anscombe's Account of the Practical Syllogism".
The Philosophical Review. Vol. LXXI, No. 4. (October 1962):
448-461.

Mullane, Harvey. "Psychoanalytic Explanation and Rationality". The
Journal of Philosophy. Vol. LXVIII, No. 14 (July 22, 1971):
413-426.

Nagel, Thomas. The Possibility of Altruism. Oxford: The Clarendon
Press, 1970.

_____. "War and Massacre". Philosophy and Public Affairs.
Vol. 1, No. 2 (Winter 1972): 123-144.

Quine, Willard Van Orman. "Two Dogmas of Empiricism". In From a Logical
Point of View. Cambridge: Harvard University Press, 1961.

Rorty, Richard. "Incorrigibility as the Mark of the Mental". The
Journal of Philosophy. Vol. LXVII, No. 12 (June 25, 1970): 399-424.

Ryle, Gilbert. The Concept of Mind. New York: Barnes and Noble, 1949.

Santas, Gerasimos. "Aristotle on Practical Inference, the Explanation
of Action, and Akrasia". Phronesis. Vol. XIV, No. 2. (1969): 178-192.

_____. "Plato's Protagoras and Explanations of Weakness". The
Philosophical Review. Vol. LXXV, No. 1. (1966): 3-33.

Schopenhauer, Arthur. *Essays on the Freedom of the Will*. Edited and translated by Konstantin Kolenda. New York: Liberal Arts Press, 1960

Scheffler, Israel. *The Anatomy of Inquiry*. New York: The Library of Liberal Arts, Bobbs-Merrill Company, Inc. 1963.

Scriven, Michael. "Explanations, Predictions, and Laws". In *Minnesota Studies in the Philosophy of Science*. Vol. III. Edited by Herbert Feigl and Grover Maxwell. Minneapolis: University of Minnesota Press, 1962.

Sidgewick, Henry. "Unreasonable Action". In *Mind*. New Series Vol. 2 (1893): 174-187.

Slote, M.A. "Free Will, Determinism, and the Theory of Important Criteria". *Inquiry*. Vol. 12, No. 3. Autumn 1969.

Stoutland, Frederick. "The Causal Theory of Action". In *Essays on Explanation and Understanding*. Edited by Huha Manninen and Raimo Tuomela. Dordrecht, Holland: D. Reidel Publishing Company, 1976.

Taylor, Charles. *The Explanation of Behaviour*. London: Routledge and Kegan Paul, 1964.

Taylor, Richard. "I Can". *The Philosophical Review*. Vol. LXIX No. 1 (1960): 78-89.

Von Wright, Georg Henrik. *Explanation and Understanding*. Ithaca: Cornell University Press, 1971.

Walsh, James J. *Aristotle's Conception of Moral Weakness*. New York: Columbia University Press, 1963.

Watson, Gary. "The Nature of Responsibility". Unpublished Ph.D. dissertation. Princeton University, 1972.

White, Morton. "Positive Freedom, Negative Freedon and Possibility". *The Journal of Philosophy*. Vol. LXX, No. 11 (June 7, 1973): 309-317.

Winter, Judith. "The Concept of Energy in Psychoanalytic Theory". *Inquiry*. Vol. 14, Nos. 1-2 (Summer 1971): 138-146.

Wittgenstein, Ludwig. *Philosophical Investigations*. Translated by G.E.M. Anscombe. Oxford: Basil Blackwell, 1963.

Wright, Larry. "Functions". *The Philosophical Review*. Vol. LXXXII, No. 2 (April 1973): 139-168.

For Product Safety Concerns and Information please contact our EU
representative GPSR@taylorandfrancis.com
Taylor & Francis Verlag GmbH, Kaufingerstraße 24, 80331 München, Germany

www.ingramcontent.com/pod-product-compliance
Lightning Source LLC
Chambersburg PA
CBHW071824300426

44116CB00009B/1434